TULIP'S BUBBLE

The Economics behind Cultural Fads and Trends

Tulip Mittal

INDIA · SINGAPORE · MALAYSIA

Notion Press Media Pvt Ltd

No. 50, Chettiyar Agaram Main Road,
Vanagaram, Chennai, Tamil Nadu – 600 095

First Published by Notion Press 2021
Copyright © Tulip Mittal 2021
All Rights Reserved.

ISBN 978-1-68538-262-9

This book is dedicated to
Mom,
Dad,
and my brother, Aushim.

CONTENTS

PROLOGUE

Drawn to the concept of "Tulip's Bubble" (in part due to its similarity with my given name), I began researching more such "bubbles" of the past. I had always heard how different fads have economic implications, especially when it comes to volatile commodities, but I never really understood what truly transpired. In unravelling the socioeconomic implications of Tulip's Bubble and other similar phenomenon, my learning extended to other historically famous ones, such as the Dotcom Bubble, the Housing Bubble etc., until I stumbled upon some quirky, unconventional ideas, that in turn, led to one unifying theme.

As an avid reader and a religious follower of the contemporary fad culture, I decided to jot down trends and fads that have arisen over the past few years since I felt these would be more relatable to me and my target audience. What fascinated me more, however, were the economic principles surrounding these trends. Often, I found myself wondering in hindsight: what really happens during a fad?

Indeed, a particular product or service becomes extremely popular, but what leads to its downfall? Is the business environment instrumental in influencing the cultural preferences for a certain time period? Or is it the opposite? Or are the two entwined? And how does it affect those who're actively engaged in making the fad a success? Seeking answers, I decided to study and decode underlying theories and prospective effects intensively. Eventually, I chronicled my findings in this book for my fellow teenagers to demystify seemingly complex economic concepts vis-a-vis popular trends.

Often, we come across some terms that seem quite vague and complex, especially when they are technical. Keeping that in mind, I realized that some of my readers too might find certain economic terms/concepts really confusing, so I've tried my best to elaborate on the basics. This book is a serious yet light-hearted approach towards economics. My attempts to establish a conversational tone throughout the book were intentional since I want to eradicate the image in the minds of people, of economics being a difficult subject that only academically-oriented people can comprehend. The personal tone felt really intimate and important to me; hence I've used it throughout.

I am deeply captivated by the multi-faceted dimensions surrounding basic fads and trends and have gained unprecedented amounts of knowledge and experience while composing this book - the best way of representing a piece of me to my readers.

I hope you love reading this book as much as I did writing it!

Tulip.

ACKNOWLEDGEMENTS

This book took an immense amount of work and it would not exist without the invaluable contributions of a number of incredibly thoughtful and supportive people.

I am thankful to my parents who have been my guiding light throughout the journey of writing my book, from reading early drafts to offering insights and encouragement. Many times when I was uncertain about being able to deliver a meaningful, substantial book, they constantly motivated me to take it day by day. Thank you Mom and Dad, for everything you have done for me. A special thank you to my brother Aushim who has been my pillar of strength and encouraged me at all times.

I owe my interest in pursuing Economics on a professional domain to my Economics teachers, at Delhi Public School, R.K.Puram. The way they taught us in class really captured my interest in this subject as they simplified the most difficult concepts and explained them in the most exciting manner.

This work drives inspiration from my school Principal, Ms. Padma Srinivasan, a leading educationist. All my school teachers and mentors have been extremely helpful throughout my journey, and I would like to bestow my heartiest gratitude to them.

WHAT ARE FADS?

Heard of the flared pants or the Adidas superstars that every teenager flaunts? Or of the mannequin challenge? If yes, it is safe to say that you have also been an active member of the fad culture, which can influence the masses globally.

What does the term fad mean? In layman's terms, a fad can be described as a period of intense popularity of a particular object, activity, lifestyle, etc. These usually last for a given period, and the sudden realization about the ordinary nature of these fads leads to its decline. History has seen the vast scope of fads from fashion to titles to food items. If you belong to my generation of locked-down individuals, you must have also seen the incredible *Dalgona coffee* fad, which convinced the most stoic individuals to display their artistic talents!

Types of fads:

Object Fads – These are items that people purchase even though they have little value or practical use. Examples include hula hoops, Cabbage Patch Kids, Pokemon games, toys, trading cards, clothes, and snack foods [1].

Activity Fads – These are not about objects, rather about activities undertaken. Include pursuits such as wacky hairstyles, body piercing, or flash mobs [1].

Idea Fads – Idea fads revolve around a particular ideology rather than an activity or object. These are new-age thoughts and ideas and can range from astrology to occult [1].

Personality Fads – These are fads that centre around a celebrity for a short period. For instance, the hype for Milli-Vanilli or Eminem. [1].

No one tells you that, oh look, this is a new fad. You observe it. Companies search for means to capitalize on it. For instance, scrunchies - the typical VSCO girl hair ties became popular back in 2019. Small start-ups saw this as an excellent opportunity to start selling these scrunchies songs with supplementary so-called aesthetic accessories. And whoosh! No one realized that these scrunchies are no longer an obsession for people anymore. Almost all fads have a minute shelf life in this constantly evolving world. Of course, that is understandable; we humans are so dynamic and creative that we set firecrackers that light the world. Soon, once this firecracker reaches everyone, the value is degraded because these objects or services no longer have the unique factor. The smoke consumes it all.

Now, you might wonder, if a particular fad for a product persists at a large scale, do we again get dragged into the demand-supply problem? Yes, absolutely! As more and more people start demanding these products, the prices rise and as a result, people start looking for substitutes. Often, the fad culture leads to black marketing since miscellaneous players enjoy reaping supernormal profits at the expense of naive consumers.

Many times, it transpires that fads are here to stay. Just because they get overruled by other fads or silently recede away from the public limelight does not mean that they disappear entirely. No, sometimes they get embedded into our minds as some sort of tradition. For instance, Hula-Hoops in the 1950s and Frisbees in the 1960s were popular fads that have now become common place items for people belonging even to the 21st century. Another popular fad that transitioned into a tradition is a piñata, a tearable bag hung on the ceiling for celebration. Usually, in India, young children try to catch hold of this bag that promises goodies on their birthdays. This tradition has a new shape now: piñata cakes. These are very appealing and innovative in the sense that when a person breaks the hard outer covering of this cake, it breaks only to reveal the soft, tempting layers of cake it beholds. Forgive me for all this imagery, I too want to try this out now! So, either way, a piñata is used for the concept of celebration despite the form it acquires.

Thus, fads are often momentary periods of excitement for a product, service, or lifestyle adaptation. Still, they might turn out to be everlasting sometimes. As long as people like you and I engage in cool, trendy activities, fads will continue occurring.

WHAT ARE TRENDS?

You certainly must have heard the word trend. But what is a trend? Does it have a meaning outside the boring trendlines you read in your high school/college textbooks? Let us discuss a few characteristics of trends. According to the Cambridge dictionary, a trend is "a general development or change in a situation or in the way that people are behaving" [1]. Trends have a very long lifespan, and that is because they serve a purpose that continues to be in demand and point at a permanent shift in the market/world. They are primarily driven by consumer needs and build their popularity over time [4]. Trends thrive because of deep-seated social, political, and environmental factors [2].

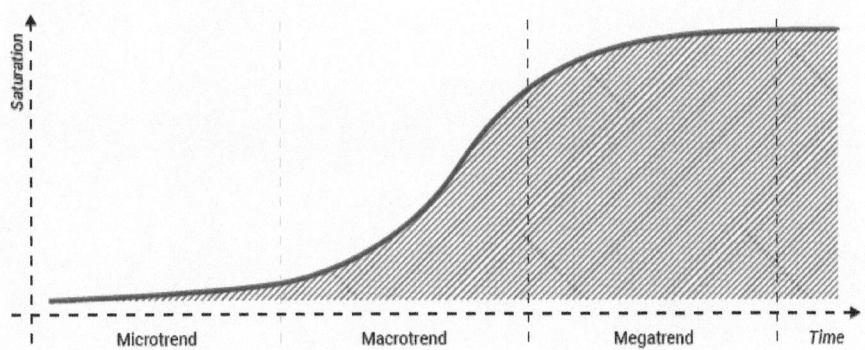

Types of Trends [7]

Mega-trends are events shaping different aspects of life that occur throughout an extended period. One can say that these events are prodded as a reaction to the behaviour and activities of people in the past. For instance, urbanization and climate change would fall in this category.

Macro-trends are a subset of mega-trends. In other words, there can be various macrotrends under a single larger mega-trend. Because of the considerable size and scope of mega-trends, macro-trends focus on certain parts of the mega-trends. For an Apple stock, a macro-trend would be the trends of various stock parameters such as free cash flow, price to earnings ratio, etc.

Micro-trends are essentially subsets of macro-trends. Within a single macro-trend, there can be numerous micro-trends. These are known to be lengthy, diverse, and active. An example of a micro-trend would be when Bitcoin became a famous cryptocurrency.

Trends usually possess agility, have identifiable and explainable rises (rise slowly in most cases) [5]. An example of a trend is the rise in the number of people starting to trade in decentralized cryptocurrencies post-pandemic, owing to its many advantages over legacy monetary systems. Problem-solving plays a vital role in trends, and this problem solving ensures the longevity of the trends [3].

ECONOMICS AND CULTURAL BEHAVIOUR

Source of Image: Left [1], Right [2]

Choices. What are they based on? We find certain goods or services appealing. But why? Is it our inner voice shaping our preferences? Do we always really consider whether we are engaging in rational choices? Or is it that the people around us find something exceptional, which naturally makes it appealing to us. Yes, external factors like the environment, religion, and culture often influence our desires, preferences, and outlook in life. Do they influence economic behaviour and vice versa? Certainly [3].

Economic culture consists of the attitudes, beliefs, and values that influence people's economic activities in society. Indeed, different geographical conditions, beliefs, norms, and values that pass on from one generation to the next and across social interactions shape individual preferences. Cultural economics also highlights that generational customs and values affect the present economic decisions [4].

So what is influenced by what? Culture by economics or economics by culture? A safe answer would be that the two are pretty much interlinked. There is not an absolute side to it.

Often, economics influences culture. For instance, a particular religion might advocate that the women in the household are not supposed to work as per the cultural norms of the society. However, if, let's say the man of the house passes away and there is no one to earn the livelihood, the woman will step up and work to sustain the family. Hey, working, using resources, producing output, earning income to fulfil needs and desires in life sounds very…economic-y. Moreover, notice, this woman's decision is conflicting with the cultural norms but isn't survival the ultimate goal?

Let's take another instance of this interlink. Globalization. How does it affect culture? It brings the culture of two or more countries closer [5]. The introduction of McDonald's in India was a significant step towards Indians adopting the Western world's eating habits, i.e., fast food. The sacred Mac burger, as we know and relish today, was a big bomb even then. Indian families always had the culture of eating home-cooked, fresh food, which would ensure nutritional fulfilment. However, McDonald's opened the possibility of a plethora of new types of fast food items that triggered the taste buds of Indian consumers. Keeping in mind the cultural tastes of Indian society, McDonald's altered the menu by replacing beef items with chicken. It achieved economies of scale since standardized potato and chicken patties could be produced at a large scale in their automated production systems, which resemble assembly lines. Additionally, procurement of raw materials in bulk contributed to cost reductions. Here, we see how economics and culture are interlinked. One influences the other.

So in today's time, we all are interconnected via globalization, and it makes sense to make wise economic decisions given the cultural factors that influence our opinion.

1

TULIP'S BUBBLE

Bubbles. What are they? *She thinks we don't know what soap bubbles are, huh.* Well, I am not talking about those kinds of bubbles. However, they have a similar effect in economic terms: you fall when there are too many because they are slippery.

So what does an economic bubble refer to? Let's go step by step. Imagine you see a pretty rouge cape in the flea market. You want it. What is the price, you ask. *Today's your lucky day ma'am, you place a price on it!* Oh lovely, I will buy it for ₹100. No, I can pay you ₹130, chimes in a young lad. Sir, I can pay ₹190, chimes another. And another will pay ₹250. And then, all of a sudden, a huge crowd quarrels to buy the cape, which eventually drives up the price to ₹600. There, it's purchased. Now, this last bidder will try to sell the cape for even higher, thereby making a sweet profit. But then comes a wise lady who points out how this cap is probably worth just ₹50. Mind you, she did a quick analysis and has a valid argument. Who wants the cape now? No one. So now that this cape lies with someone who bought it for ₹600, he will want to sell it - to get rid of it. But it's basically valueless, so no one is going to buy it from him. Imagine this setting, where a larger group of buyers and sellers are involved. They will all suffer because owning an asset with practically no value will fetch them no wealth.

Putting this in economic terms, an economic bubble is a phenomenon in which an asset is overvalued to such an extent that when it bursts i.e. the prices fall, it causes considerable losses in the market and can result in HUGE debts. A famous bubble would be the United States Housing bubble of 2008 which led to a deep recession.

Why do these bubbles arise? Greed? *Check.* Trendy? *Check.* The temptation to sell these assets at a higher price to make profits? *Check.* No valid reason? *Check.* We refer to this overenthusiasm by investors, causing a massive rise in prices, as *irrational exuberance,* a term coined by Alan Greenspan.

Where are these bubbles coming from? How do they arise?

When the economy is expanding, there is a greater amount of money flowing (liquidity) through the economy. This means that the cost of borrowing, i.e., the interest rates payable, falls, so investors want to borrow more naturally. Subsequently, they invest this borrowed capital in other assets such as commodities and real estate. In the case that a large number of investors invest money in a limited number of assets, prices will rise. Now, you imagine this at a macro-level, and there you have, a glistening bubble [1].

The onset of the Dutch golden age saw a dramatic rise in demand for Tulips, which were sold from anywhere between 3000 to 4000 florins, the Dutch currency in the 17th century.

Tulip Mania - it literally translates to mania about Tulips. It all started in the 17th century in the Dutch economy, when a single Tulip flower was even more valuable than some houses! Investors got caught in the excitement of making abnormal profits. Many of them had a vision that was clouded by greed. They never anticipated that the cost of this thrill was mass bankruptcy: the bubble finally burst in 1637.

There were several types of Tulips, of which *Semper Augustus* was the most valuable. It became so widely demanded that after a certain point of time, only 12 remained. Since there was a supply shortage, the man who held a monopoly over the Tulips sold them at 13000 florins - this amount was almost equal to a house! Thus, due to the exorbitantly high prices, the demand for these flowers fell. The prices started falling, leading to a crash in the Tulip market in The Netherlands [2].

Another reason why the Tulip market is believed to have crashed is that many people bought these bulbs on credit, hoping that they could liquidate these when the prices soar higher and thus repay their debts. However, as the prices crashed, these people were forced to liquidate the bulbs at any price possible to evade complete bankruptcy.

Gradually, in the 19th century, from being a thing of beauty to a prized possession, Tulips became the very source of survival for the Dutch population: they relied on Tulip bulbs for food. Caught in a deadly famine during the second world war, a starving population found hope in the abundance of Tulips grown on large farmlands.

Furthermore, the nutritional value they possessed raised the hopes of the future utility of this bulb. Presently, they are still consumed and enjoyed, especially because of their sweet-tasting petals [3].

The main concern I have with such bubbles is that there is yet to be a proper mechanism that can help in curbing these bubbles. Some economists believe that employing a contractionary monetary policy of increasing the federal reserve rate, which is the rate that a commercial bank has to pay to the bank it is borrowing from on an overnight basis, would discourage banks from borrowing and lead to a decrease in the money supply. Interest rates would rise, discouraging the public from borrowing from banks, which might deter credit booms that contribute to bubbles [1]. However, until there is more clarity on how to avoid getting trapped by the bubble, an investor can watch out for signs that give rise to a bubble. Take a step back and see what transpires.

2

INSTAGRAM REELS – THE NEXT INDIAN TIKTOK

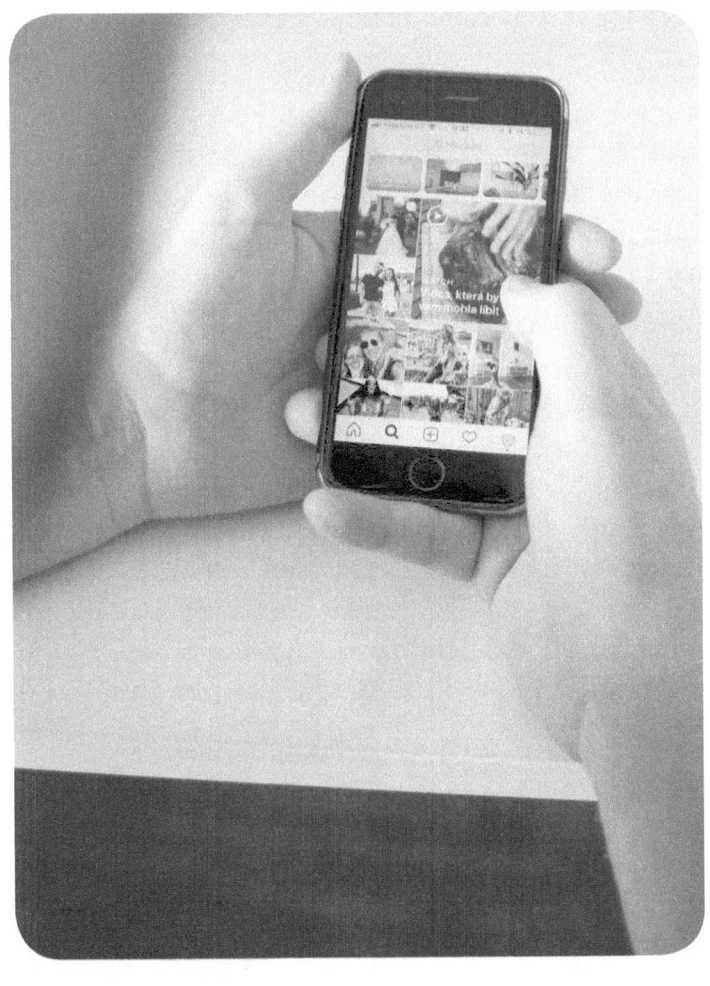

What happens when we get obsessed with a particular fad? And what if that fad is related to technology which is extremely dynamic? Consider that this technology is controlled by a neighbouring country that is a rival. Well, things are bound to turn ugly. First things first, you should know what I'm talking about... every teenager's pass-time: TikTok. This app was established by Bytedance, a Chinese tech giant. Launched in 2016, TikTok surpassed almost 200 million downloads by Indian users before its ban [1].

The literal craze behind this app was because of its ability to sway even the laziest of people - once they laid fingers on the app. If you are unaware of what it does, keep reading on to discover how your average teenage child became an internet sensation over just a month!

This app allows the user to make short, fun, quirky, and off-beat videos using songs from many genres. So you can create a dance while there is a Taylor Swift song playing in the background. And now, when the user hits the "upload" button and manages to get more than a million views from a large network of audience, she can earn instant fame and money!

Coming back to the introduction, during the Covid lockdown, people all over the world started relying on TikTok as a means of entertainment. Given that TikTok support 15 local Indian languages, everyone - from a celebrity to a nurse to a roadside vendor - had equal access to this platform that could cater to a diverse audience [9]. It gave many artists - dancers, musicians, comedians, and actors - a platform to reach out to all socio-economic classes. People started becoming social media sensations. As a result, more and more companies and small businesses began approaching these rising stars to promote their products. And voila! Your little girl is already buying her own clothes.

However, in June 2020, this fad soon crashed in India, as due to the geopolitical tensions with China, the Indian government banned 59 Chinese apps - including TikTok. Capitalizing on this opportunity, Instagram launched a new feature called "Reels," which is an almost equivalent version of TikTok. Reels is a feature that enables an individual to record videos, in which custom audio, filters, and effects can be incorporated, that last for about 15-30 seconds [3]. Diminishing attention spans and the void left by TikTok made the public pounce at this new feature, so people started making reels for fun. Now, don't you worry about those influencers who were making money because of TikTok. They had another outlet to do so: Reels. Gaining popularity directly on Instagram again initiated this cycle of brands and promotion. So it seems Indian influencers had nothing to lose. However, Bytedance sure had a loss of $6 Billion, according to estimates by a recent report [1].

How do these influencers contribute to the economy? Social platforms like Instagram, Facebook, and YouTube tend to attract influencers who gain a large number of followers. As per Marketing Hub, Instagram has conquered the position of the most attractive platform for such influencers. About 79% of brands try Instagram influencer campaigns, as compared with Facebook (46%) and YouTube (36%) [4].

Influencer marketing has served as a huge cost-cutter for firms as they no longer need to spend incredible amounts of money on magazines and other media advertisements. Earlier, a major portion of corporate marketing budgets included expenditure on billboards and magazines. However, people probably started ignoring these media to a certain extent because companies could never access such a wide audience before, as they have been able to with Instagram.

Paid advertisements and collaborations were always a part of Instagram marketing. However, with the help of reels, gaining traction is a lot easier on this platform now. A 20% increase in Indian Instagram users was observed in October 2020 which was partly due to reels [1]. What's more, in India, the average time spent on reels spiked by 3.5% [3]. If you are not yet well-versed about reels marketing, maybe you need to reconsider your marketing strategies!

Targeting specific communities, these reels have the effect of converting advertisement viewers to consumers. For instance, Indian Ethnic Co., an Indian ethnic wear company based in Mumbai, saw a rise in turnover from ₹30 lakh in March to ₹65 lakh in June 2020. The company credited Reels as a major contributor to this success [8]! Possibly, this trend has led to more and more consumers increasing their consumption of clothes, fast food, watches, FMCGs, and services. Moreover, many companies have started investing more in deals with such influencers, given the positive outcomes of influencer marketing in the past. For instance, Daniel Wellington - a luxury watches' brand - had seen success in the period of 2013 to 2015, owing to its innovative marketing strategy of gifting influencers watches, hoping to get more exposure to their brand!

Thus, an increase in India's aggregate demand and real GDP can be predicted due to such a sudden increase in consumption and investment [5].

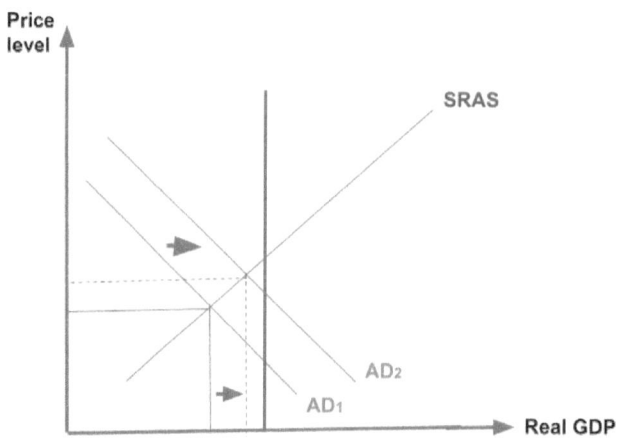

IMPACT OF INSTAGRAM REELS ON AGGREGATE DEMAND AND REAL GDP

Topping the charts of highest paid Indian influencers, Virat Kohli, a phenomenal Indian cricketer, is paid almost ₹5 crores per each promotional post he shares. Even if someone who has 500,000 followers promotes reputed brands, they could earn an average of ₹1.2 lakh per post.

While there is no hard and fast secret formula, per se, to becoming a huge hit in a short duration, the ability to optimize one's potential via Reels is a great step towards successful engagement, given that the content created is entertaining and is targeted at the right audience. From the perspective of both users and businesses, Reels seems to be a win-win feature!

3

MEMEONOMICS

Source of Image: [4]

Ever heard of 'Stonks'? What about 'Success Kid'? Or 'Shut Up and Take my Money'? If you have replied in the affirmative to one or more of these questions, then you, my friend, are a member of the meme world. Most millennials and Gen-Z people recognize, share, and enjoy memes. For anyone *(in the baby boomer generation)* who has no idea about what memes are, a meme is (and I quote Lexico) "an image, video, piece of text, etc., typically humorous in nature, that is copied and spread rapidly by internet users, often with slight variations" [6]. They denote humour, derision, satire, are relatable and act as conversation starters, and from a business point of view – quirky enough for people to appreciate them and engage with the product/offering.

Memes are especially useful for companies as they not only help in spreading their popularity but also act as mediums of market research. There are professional meme creators – people with a plethora of creative mental outlets who stay up to date with the latest social media trends and monetize them for businesses. I repeat, meme creation is an actual profession! Many companies are transitioning towards memes to reach out to the youth since *humour is the most attractive quality, isn't it?* A study revealed that a freelancing meme maker can earn up to $2600 annually by sharing creative and interactive memes [8]. Many brands are getting attuned to this type of marketing, given its ability to gather traction on social media at lower costs. For instance, an internationally renowned luxury fashion brand, Gucci, gauged the success of memes by releasing a #TFWgucci project which received massive engagement [9]. Talking about innovation, our very own Nickelodeon saw the fad about Spongebob Squarepants' memes and literally converted those to collectibles! [10].

Source of Image: [2]

Let us dissect the above meme.

Opportunity cost is defined as "the value of the next-highest-valued alternative use of that resource" [7]. A simple example explaining this is that of a doctor. Let us consider that he lives in Maryland. Due to the demand for doctors due to the pandemic, he got two job offers – one worth $75,000 in New York City and one worth $70,000 in San Francisco. Considering his preferences and other factors, he went with the New York City one. He will be earning $75,000, and his opportunity cost will be $70,000, i.e., the next best alternative. What the above meme is trying to convey is that Netflix, the famous over-the-top (OTT) platform, is the next best alternative to going to class. College students have a reputation for watching shows on Netflix for hours at a time, and hence, the meme.

GameStop and AMC. Do these words ring a bell? If they don't, open Reddit to search r/WallStreetBets, and buy those stocks if you dare! Both GameStop and AMC are (at the time of writing) examples of meme stocks. Let me give a brief insight into them. These stocks were heavily shorted (bet against, presumably due to lack of sound financial indicators) on the stock market. One fine day, some Jim's and Chad's on r/WallStreetBets decided to pump up the prices of the stocks. This was primarily done as revenge against hedge funds because the general public held them accountable for the 2008 financial crisis. To add insult to injury, these hedge funds even received billions of dollars of taxpayer's money as a bailout.

As a result of their memes, the hedge funds that shorted these stocks were short squeezed. Short squeezing is a scenario when a company suffers losses when they bet against another company, and the share price of the company unanticipatedly goes up. As a result, the hedge funds lost billions of dollars. The obvious winners were the thousands of people who bought the stock at a low price and sold them until the prices of GameStop/AMC were quite high. This became international headlines, and the widespread use of memes and the cult-like following of the Redditors genuinely shook many hedge funds. This entire saga (for the GameStop share) is called GameStop mania and shows the impact memes can have in the real business world?. A meme showing the pumping of such stocks and the mindset of many people is seen below.

Source of Image: [5]

Let's discuss the meme industry cycle. Memes have been around since the 2000s, but those were limited and not mainstream. If I remember correctly, memes became popular worldwide in 2015, when everyone first started sharing them on social media platforms. Ever since, memes have been in a somewhat boom phase – the first part of an economic cycle. There has been high demand, and the supply has been ample too. Why you may ask. Well, people always seek relatable humour and witty forms of media. And the perennial supply? Don't worry about that!

As long as we humans have the quest for expressing creativity, the meme communities will never fail us with their fantastic, ubiquitous memes! Will this fad ever bust? In my honest opinion, I thought the rise of substitutes - short video apps, such as Instagram Reels and TikTok - would signal an end to memes' popularity. But that has not been the case. These short video apps integrate effectively with memes to make content even more wholesome for people. Do memes follow an economic cycle? That remains to be seen. But in the meme-time, just open your Facebook/ Instagram/Twitter, and laugh at a few memes by the world's richest man, AKA Elon Musk, on Dogecoin [1].

4

PODCAST – A FUTURE BROADCAST?

Source of Image: [1]

"Saira, I can't show my face. You know how camera conscious I get." Why can't I simply deliver my voice to the audience somehow?

"What 'audience' Kylah? You're practically catering to just maybe fifteen high school kids!"

"Still, I hate recording while showing my face...you know it. Ensuring that I have proper expressions is so tiresome..help me out!"

"Why don't you try making podcasts? I've heard that it's really easy to get traction through them."

"What are podcasts?"

"You are living in 2021. You should know this! But here, I'll explain it to you. According to Lexico, a podcast is "a digital audio file made available on the internet for downloading to a computer or mobile device, typically available as a series, new instalments of which can be received by subscribers automatically"[3].

"I don't get this bookish definition. You've got to do better, Saira!"

"Podcasts are audio chats, primarily in the form of episodes that focus on a particular topic of discussion. So, assume that you want to talk about the different biological phenomena that exist. All you have to do is release a podcast which is divided into different episodes. Each episode can describe a different phenomenon, and you can even bring guests on board to talk about certain subjects. It can be pretty informal because the idea of a podcast is to establish a conversational tone to grab the audience's interest. One doesn't require a kindle or a DVD player to listen to them - they are typically heard on smartphones and can be either paid or free. Nowadays, podcast creators upload their podcasts on as many platforms as possible to attract a larger audience. For instance, platforms like Spotify, Apple Podcasts, and Google podcasts are popular in today's time."

"Is this a new concept? Tell me more!"

"Not really...this concept was first introduced in 2004 by Adam Curry and Dave Weiner by designing a program called iPodder that downloaded radio broadcasts to an Apple iPod (Podcast got its name from **iPod** + Broad**cast**) [4]. These podcasts were quite popular during their early years (from around 2005 - 2007), but soon lost steam due to the emergence of other technologies."

"So how come podcasts are getting famous again? What is its USP (unique selling point)?"

"That is a combination of broadly five factors, namely resilience, trust, scale, effectiveness, and flexibility [5]. After the Covid pandemic, one of the pros of podcasts especially stands out - flexibility, which is the ability to listen to podcasts anywhere, anytime (one does need just an internet connection). The pandemic is shifting human attitudes and behaviours by making them want things that provide them more comfort and that are aligned with their interests, with podcasts being a 2-in-1 of those."

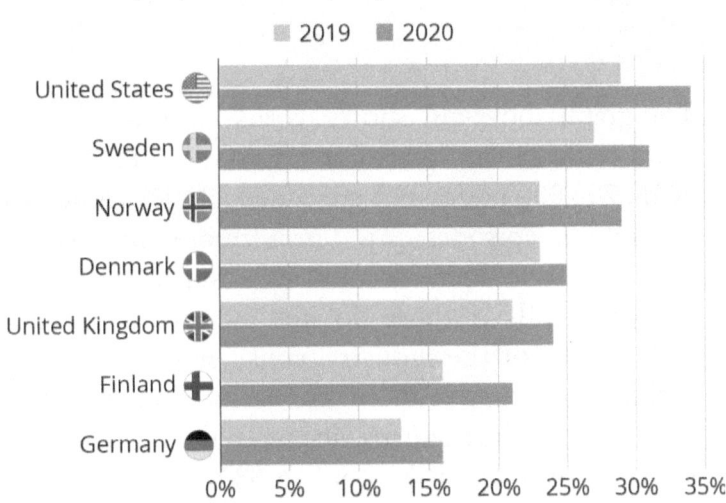

Podcasts Rising in Prominence

Share of people that listen to podcasts on a weekly basis

Based on the responses of over 14,000 adults.
Source: AudienceProject

Podcasts have been rising in popularity of late. The above graph by Statista [2] shows the number of people listening to podcasts weekly in 7 countries of the western world.

Some talking points:

♦ Finland showed an increase of 31%, the highest of all countries surveyed. In general, all 7 nations showed an increase in the number of people listening to podcasts weekly [2].

♦ The United States had the highest number of respondents who listened to podcasts at least once weekly. Now, more than half of all Americans have listened to a podcast [7].

Podcast Advertising Revenue, 2015 - 2021 (in millions)

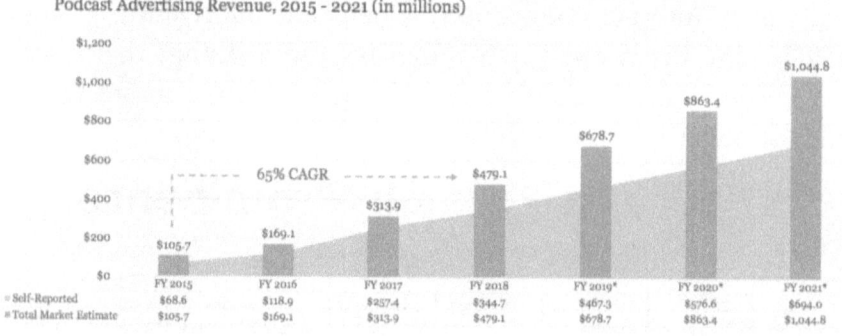

	FY 2015	FY 2016	FY 2017	FY 2018	FY 2019*	FY 2020*	FY 2021*
Self-Reported	$68.6	$118.9	$257.4	$344.7	$467.3	$576.6	$694.0
Total Market Estimate	$105.7	$169.1	$313.9	$479.1	$678.7	$863.4	$1,044.8

♦ The graph above [6] shows us that advertisement revenue from podcasts has scaled at a CAGR of 65% from 2015-2018. 700,000 podcasts were added in 2019 alone, with over 29 million episodes [6]. Furthermore, podcast listening numbers have increased by 42% since the start of the pandemic [8]. If these do not indicate the massive size and growth of the industry, consider how the big tech is rushing to monetize these. The latest news is that Amazon is purchasing the exclusive license to the famous "Smartless" podcast for a deal valued up to $80 million. This for sure ought to turn your head [9].

How does the economics of podcasts work? Well, it really does depend on differing scenarios, but let's talk about a couple of them.

The first is based on a subscription model, i.e. users pay a fixed monthly/weekly fee to listen to podcasts by their favourite content creators. This is a popular method, but podcasters usually need to have engaging content and be famous to have a higher consumer lifetime value and earn through this route. Remember, no one wants to pay for boring content!

Another way in which podcast content makers make money is when they earn huge revenues from advertisers. Metrics such as CPM (Cost per Mille or Thousand is the amount that the advertising company will pay to the podcast host/company upon a thousand views/listens) deduce the engagement rate and popularity levels. One more economic reason big companies are jumping on the podcasting bandwagon is simply the name and recognition that a brand can get. A case in point is Amazon's purchase of the above-mentioned 'Smartless' podcast. Although people may have a point that a fee up to $80 million is simply too high, Amazon will be able to drive most of the devoted listeners of the podcast Smartless from other platforms to Amazon Music. This, in turn, will help and fuel Amazon Music's growth, thus making sense economically.

"So, what does the future hold for podcasts?"

Given the rapid evolution of demand for new types of media, and the accessibility quotient they offer, podcasts might be a hit even in the upcoming generations. An underrated facet of podcasts is that it is better for a human's eyes! With a rapidly globalizing and technologically advancing world, most of us are sitting in front of a laptop/mobile/television for hours, which is not the best thing in the long run. So if a person can listen to podcasts, they won't be straining their eyes. Apart from that, many previously not so well-off parts of the world are developing, with growing internet subscriptions. If companies and individuals can reach out to these vast audiences through tailor-made podcasts, that indeed would herald a new era for the growth and development of podcasts.

Despite not entailing a visual representation of any sort, one can see the bright future of podcasts!

5

OTT – Are Viewers Chilling?

Source of Image: [3]

L *ockdown 2020. Bored in a house, in a house bored.* Sitting at home, what means of entertainment do you adopt? Netflix! This represents the thoughts of 16 million individuals, just during the lockdown, as per a report by BBC News. Netflix is one of the many popular OTT platforms that are thriving in India as of 2021 [2].

But what do we mean by OTT platforms? The acronym stands for over-the-top platforms, which get their name from the idea that they do not follow the conventional satellite TV platforms. Instead, the streaming is literally "over the top" of these via the internet. More than a couple of them have captured the Indian audience - Netflix, Hotstar, Amazon Prime, Voot, etc.

How these platforms work is that anyone with a stable internet connection and a smartphone, laptop, or tablet can watch whichever show, movie, or web series they prefer. I find it pretty convenient because I do not have to wait for Sunday to watch the sequel of Avengers. And let's not forget the ad-free aspect. A boon for anti-ad maniacs for sure, myself included!

However, this freedom to opt for streaming services benefits primarily only consumers. The television companies now have to deal with this competition from OTTs because, hey, the consumers can devote their precious time streaming only one of the two mediums. And when it is not TV that they choose, the broadcasters will certainly not be happy. Moreover, this also hurts the advertisement industry because there is no way to convert viewers to potential buyers of their product if they switch to OTTs. Thus, the local entertainment industry is not at a gain when it comes to OTTs.

For instance, as per a report by Variety, owing to OTTs, TV, and satellite companies have lost about 6 million subscribers in 2019 in the USA. In India in 2019, television subscriptions dropped by about 26 million, of which at least 0.3-0.4 million subscribers might have evolved to OTTs [1]. This translates to substantial revenue losses for not only television broadcasting houses but also for cinemas. People have the option of waiting for a set window of time to watch the new releases sitting at home.

My uncle, a movie buff, always has this perception that shifting to Amazon Prime is more cost-effective than going to cinemas. Why is that? Well, he counts every single penny he is spending, and this is what his expenditure on a movie experience in the cinema hall looks like:

Cost of Movie tickets (for 2)	₹900
Back row seats	₹300
Expenditure on deluxe popcorn with extra butter	₹250
Cost of fuel consumed while traveling to and fro from the cinema hall in his car	a whopping ₹200
Stopover at Natural's to buy wifey a standard Vanilla cone (double scoop)	₹300
TOTAL	₹1950

As a regular visitor to the hall, my uncle is not keen on spending ₹1950 every single time for ₹900 movie tickets. He would rather bear the fixed cost of paying the annual subscription charges for watching Amazon Prime or Netflix all year long without incurring these extra expenses.

He is the face of the typical Indian household, whose demand for video-on-demand services has been growing by more than 25% in the past two years. As per a Boston Consulting Group report, in India, the OTT industry is estimated to become $5 billion by 2023 [4]! The report further highlights that this growth requires the crucial factors to be fully developed: access to data, which India must improve, smart devices, and affluence across the remotest of regions.

This will certainly be a challenging goal to achieve, given the socioeconomic differences and the inequalities present in India.

Yet, with the proper steps to ensure equitable access to these factors, we can surely keep a positive vision for integrating OTTs in a commoner's household.

All said and done, the speed of adoption of the OTTs has been incredible. Let's wait and watch where the OTTs land up by the time this book hits bookstores!

6

SUBSCRIPTION BOXES – ANYTIME, ANYWHERE...

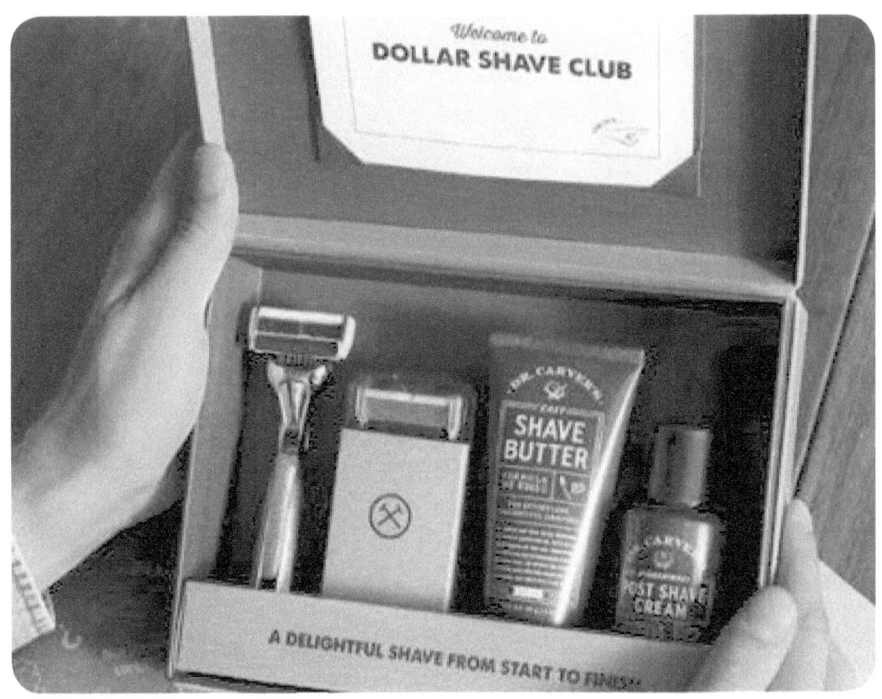

Source of Image: [6]

Subscription Boxes - What an introduction they have been to the global e-commerce market! Although people have divided opinions on their feasibility and pricing, everyone ought to praise the ingenuity and transformational potential of subscription boxes that are disrupting the gigantic and old-school retail market. So first let's begin by discussing the different kinds of subscriptions available to consumers - replenishment subscriptions, access subscriptions, and curation subscriptions. Replenishment subscriptions are those which allow people to automate purchases of certain commodities, such as automating purchases of groceries weekly. Access subscriptions are those in which customers pay a monthly fee for member-only perks or reduced prices [9]. Paid Blog viewing websites, such as Medium, is a perfect example of this.

E-commerce subscriptions, %		Key consumer value	Description	Example companies
Subscribe for replenishment	32	Save time and money	Replenish the same or similar items Primary categories are commodity items such as razors, vitamins	Amazon Subscribe & Save, Dollar Shave Club, and Ritual
Subscribe for curation	55	Be surprised by product variety	Receive a curated selection of different items, with varying levels of consumer decision making required Primary categories are apparel, food, beauty products	Birchbox, Blue Apron, and Stitch Fix
Subscribe for access	13	Gain exclusive access	Membership provides access and can convey additional "VIP" perks Primary categories are apparel, food	JustFab, NatureBox, and Thrive Market

100%

So what are subscription boxes (aka curation subscriptions)? According to Just4UBox, they are a "recurring physical delivery of curated niche-oriented products packaged in a box designed to create an experience and offer additional value on top of the actual products" [1]. Let me explain it in simpler words by giving an example. Imagine that you want shaving and grooming products and that too monthly without much hassle. *We all like a smooth chin that has a smooth process.* Enter Dollar Shave Club, a company that makes you fill out a form asking your preferences, analyses them, and curates products tailor-made to the customer's choices. They then quality package the products and ship them over to you. So you might be wondering what makes this special? The best part about this service is that it is hassle-free, and because products change monthly, there is an element of surprise... that delights the human psyche!

As with any business model, subscription boxes (a.k.a. curation subscriptions) have received both bouquets and brickbats. Some advantages of subscription boxes include convenience, customization, and potential for savings. An interesting fact regarding savings in subscription boxes is that many times a package of contents is cheaper than the total cost borne during the visit made by a customer to the retail store to purchase those contents separately [4].

On the other hand, nemesis of the subscription box model argue that customers overbuy (I would say that the problem of purchasing ancillary items is prevalent in all consumer purchases), return/exchange/quitting is difficult, and there is a certain saturation regarding the range of products sent to customers after a few months [4].

So what has the trend been for the subscription box industry? Let us analyse that from the given graph [2].

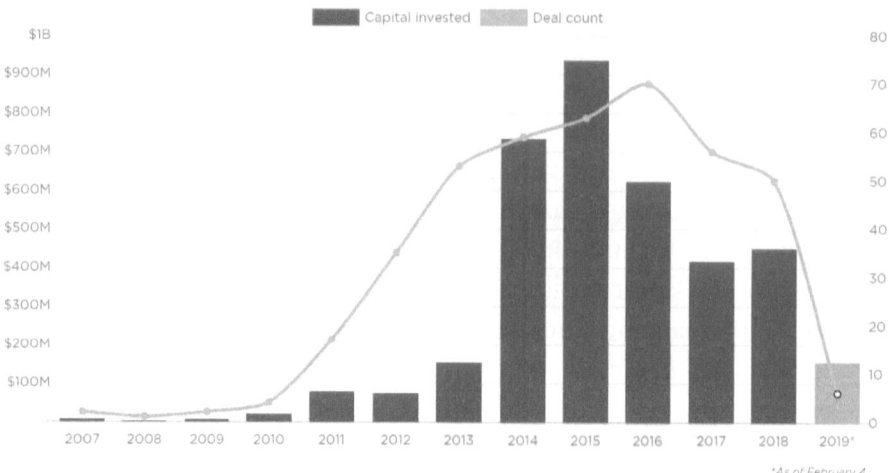

♦ The early 2010s saw a huge rise in the number of businesses using a subscription-based boxed model. The same trend was observed for venture capital investments into such businesses. This peaked in 2016, after which one could see a drop both in the number of VC deals and capital invested. However, by the end of the year 2019, the total capital invested in the subscription box industry was $1.2 billion, the rise being primarily attributed to a greater value of deals and industry maturation.

♦ According to Forbes, subscription box programs rose by over 40% a year to 3500 options, but the website traffic to subscription box retailers just rose 3% year on year for Q1-2018 against Q1- 2017, versus 10% for Q1-2017 against Q1-2016 [8].

♦ According to McKinsey, 55% of total subscriptions are curation subscriptions, with 32% and 13% subscriptions being attributed to replenishment and access subscriptions respectively [9].

These trends show that subscription boxes are here to stay. Well, you may think how does a subscription box model work from the point of view of a seller? It might seem complex but it isn't. Subscription-based model vendors use certain economic and financial metrics to determine the customer lifetime value. Customer Lifetime Value (LTV) is the key performance indicator (KPI) that effectively determines the feasibility, pricing, and business continuity of a subscription-based model [3]. From a macro point of view, the higher this metric is for all subscribers combined, the higher will be the revenue, and if the company's overall costs are lower than this combined number, that determines the company's profitability.

So what determines the future of the subscription box industry? Of course, convenience and customization will be the main drivers for customers. But as with every emerging trend of the future, technology ought to play a big role in this industry. Just consider artificial intelligence, machine learning, and big data. A customer fills in a form with their preferences, and an AI bot automatically scans the huge worldwide web for products best suited for the consumer. Humans are after all humans, and there is a limit to the data management activities that they can do. If this model does boom exponentially over the next few years, then big data and its 6 V's - volume, variety, velocity, veracity, value, and variability [6] will become crucial in the implementation of smart decision-making for future subscription box vendors.

7

THE CRAZE BEHIND NFTs

Source of Image: [5]

NFTs, or nonfungible tokens, are cryptographic tokens that allow us to purchase the unique ownership of digital assets like digital art, music, games, and even tweets! [3]

The first time you probably heard the term NFTs might have been in 2012. Of course, I do not expect my Gen Z peers to be aware of NFTs at that stage. This was the year when the first NFT was released: "Colored Coins," which were essentially like bitcoins and could represent a plethora of digital assets in the blockchain space like stocks, bonds, commodities, etc.

The second time this word caught the world's eye was in 2017, with the release of "Cryptokitties," a game that allows you to own and play with virtual cats. This game on the Ethereum blockchain saw transactions worth $1.3M within a few days of its release [1]. Such a ridiculous amount for a game that screams basic, but welcome to the world of internet fads!

More recently, in 2020, NFTs became a hype on the internet again as Dapper Labs, the developer of Cryptokitties, created virtual tokens of NBA highlights. This project - known as NBA TopShot - has seen sales up to $230 million as of February 2021. Uproars over Twitter's CEO, Jack Dorsey's attempt to sell his first tweet in March 2021 were nonchalantly ignored by the highest bidder, who put in $2.9 million and defended his purchase by calling this tweet the Mona Lisa of tweets. What this means is that he is the unique owner of this tweet, and no one in the world can buy it. Similarly, another famous music artist, Snoopp Dogg, dropped a series of NFTs in the market inspired by his journey and memories for a duration of as less as 24 hours [2]. Celebrities like Paris Hilton, Lindsay Lohan, and Shawn Mendes too gave in to this trend!

Now, with a new platform for demonstrating their talents, many musicians, comedians, and other creative professionals can finally monetize their skills by sharing their works directly with communities that appreciate them. Moreover, NFTs are extremely helpful for supporting young artists who manage to sell their art virtually in the form of tokens, as they can secure a proportion of their expected sales in advance. So today, if I sell my NFT of an artistic doughnut, I could instantly obtain 5% of my expected sales [1].

However, for digital art, NFTs are becoming extremely notorious for irrational prices. In these COVID-19 times, profits are uncertain, and income for survival is bleak for the masses. Yet many people are still buying such NFTs at exorbitant prices. For instance, recently, in 2021, digital artist Beeple sold an NFT - "Everydays — The First 5000 Days" - for $69.3 million! Similarly, The Nifty Gateway, a medium of NFT transactions, facilitated the sale of a $6 million work: Ocean Front. One could very well buy a decent house in New York for this amount. According to some experts, these prices might be unsustainable in the long run [4].

Economists describe this trend as an economic bubble, an exponential rise in market prices, and sudden crashes that cause huge economic losses (head over to the first chapter to know about the very famous Tulip's bubble!). What drives such insane prices for something as minuscule as ownership of an asset? Since the demand for nonfungible tokens is so high, and that too for one single asset, prices are bound to soar.

However, in India, there is a lack of clarity about what regulation framework NFTs classify under. As an Indian investor, the real question to consider is whether it's wise to bet so much money on an NFT, which is a concept yet to be legally validated by the government of India.

8

Bitcoin – An Asset Class or a Medium of Exchange?

Source of Image: [7]

We live in a world where needs and wants are satisfied with an accepted form of exchange, which is money. Every country has a separate fiat currency which is the country's legal tender i.e it is accepted by all.

Of late, the financial ecosystem has been undergoing a rapid transformation, led by none other than cryptocurrencies, the most popular being, bitcoin.

So what is bitcoin? It is "a decentralized digital currency, without a central bank or single administrator, that can be sent from user to user on the peer-to-peer bitcoin network without the need for intermediaries"[1]. In simple words, bitcoin is a currency built upon futuristic blockchain technology, which enhances the transparency and traceability of data. One feature unique to bitcoin is that it is entirely speculative – its value is determined collectively by people along with demand-supply factors. Unlike Gold, a somewhat relatable asset class, bitcoin has no physical products or presence. It is essentially a virtual form of exchange.

Bitcoin was created by Satoshi Nakamoto to act as a future world currency, just like the US Dollar (USD) and Indian Rupee (INR) today. For Bitcoin to act as a medium of exchange, it is expected to follow the principles of economics. But is that the case? Does it really follow economic principles? Proponents of bitcoin will say yes, while antagonists will disagree. Let us try to be completely neutral:

- ♦ **Volatility** – In simple economic terms, volatility is the measurement of the movement of a given stock/commodity/ asset. It indicates swings towards either side (gain/loss) of the purchase price. Volatility in the case of bitcoin is the rapid appreciation/depreciation of its price. If these terms seem vague to you, appreciation means when the value of the given currency, here bitcoin, increases. Whereas depreciation means that the value of the bitcoin falls. For instance, imagine a Rupee-USD scenario.

  Let's suppose, ₹75=$1

You are an Indian consumer who wants to buy the latest iPhone from the US. It costs around $1000 which means you pay ₹75,000 (not considering external factors like tariffs on imported goods etc). Suppose the value of the rupee appreciates which means it goes up to

₹60=$1

So now, you can buy the same iPhone for ₹60,000 only. The value of the rupee has increased, that is, that now you end up paying lesser for the same amount of a given good. So ideally, as an importer of iPhone, you could be happy. Depreciation also works in a similar manner.

As is the case for stocks, higher volatility indicates higher rewards when the price of a commodity appreciates and greater losses when the price of a commodity depreciates.

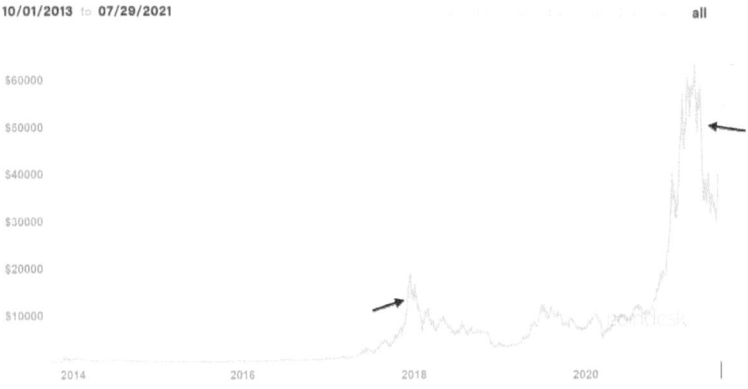

The above chart [2] shows the price of bitcoin since 2013. The left arrow drawn indicates the first-time bitcoin rapidly appreciated to reach its 2017 peak, before rapidly depreciating because of the burst of the bubble (Head over to the first chapter to know all about bubbles!). It continued to hover around the $10,000 mark after touching the trough for around 3 years until March 2020, when the coronavirus pandemic hit the world.

Investors, especially retail investors bought bitcoin at a very low price to act as a hedge (safety in case of a sudden financial loss) against the stock market. But, they didn't anticipate that the price of bitcoin would nosedive significantly owing to the worried investor sentiment. In May 2021, the value of bitcoin plummeted by half (as shown by the right arrow on the graph) because of the ban imposed by China, due to a lack of regulatory framework (and its use for unethical causes) on cryptocurrency transactions [3]. All of these ups and downs (and that too by huge amounts) indicate the volatility of bitcoin as a medium of exchange.

◆ **Supply** – The supply of bitcoin is capped at 21 million coins, which implies that no one will be able to mine bitcoin after this number is reached. Currently, around 18.5 million coins have already been mined, with just around 2.5 million more coins left to be mined. Also, even lesser numbers are in circulation because of numerous instances of people having forgotten the passwords to their private cryptocurrency wallets – essentially blocking an unspecified (but huge) number of bitcoins out of normal circulation. Now, imagine losing out on almost $220 million worth of bitcoin fortune just because you forget the password - yes we all must learn from the MASSIVE faux-pas of a German based programmer, Stefan Thomas [6]!

Adding this to the fact is that recently, institutions such as MicroStrategy and Tesla have purchased bitcoins amounting to billions of dollars. That is effectively hoarding the 'so-called future world currency'. Also, if the population and literacy level of the world continues to grow (as evident by the trends seen in India and Africa), we can expect a greater number of people vying for the same amount of bitcoin since people will have a deeper knowledge about it. This is a direct demand-supply problem because if demand increases, price increases. The demand curve will shift rightwards, which would also mean disruptions on the price of bitcoin, thus moving bitcoin away from stability and showing its volatile nature.

These points above tell us that bitcoin really is not suitable as a monetary medium of exchange. The time it takes for the confirmation of a bitcoin transaction is around 7-10 minutes, while it is a few seconds for credit/debit cards. This shows that currencies and current financial systems around the world are here to stay. As the world makes a strong economic recovery from the pandemic, consumer confidence in traditional asset classes is rising, and hence more and more people are reverting to them. Adding this to the fact that the inflation in most of the developed world is transitory, the US Dollar – undoubtedly the most powerful and influential currency on the planet is going to remain strong and bitcoin will find it hard to usurp it from its pole position.

However, there is an exception - recently, El Salvador became the first country to declare bitcoin as legal tender. There are two primary reasons for that – the country's currency was devalued in 2001 to such an extent that it had to adopt the US Dollar as its official currency. 70 percent of El Salvadorians do not have bank accounts [4], and so the parliament decided to take a futuristic future approach for the welfare of the people, and hence bitcoin. Secondly, El Salvadorians working abroad send around $4 billion a year as remittances, which is one-fifth of its Gross Domestic Product [5]. These remittances have huge wire and transactional fees, and bitcoin would eliminate that. It is too early to predict if this is a good move or not, especially because the value of bitcoin has plummeted by half due to the banning of bitcoin by the Chinese government. El Salvador is not an economy that would drastically change the landscape, but it is definitely a start.

According to me, in the long term, cryptocurrency undoubtedly has a promising future. Eventually, some sort of digital currency will become the main medium of exchange/transactions for the entire world. But is it going to be bitcoin? Just because of the fixed ceiling of supply, I would like to say no but I would surely place my bets on other revolutionary cryptocurrencies, such as Ethereum and Cardano. Whether bitcoin stays what it is right now (an asset class), or becomes what it is intended to be (medium of exchange) remains to be seen.

9

ARTWORK INVESTING – THE NEW MONEY MAKING PROPOSITION

Source of Image: [5]

Money – it's something everyone wants, and that too in unlimited quantities. Why is that – simply because every Tom, Dick, and Harry can spend it to cover bills, their wants, for enjoyment purposes, and have a lavish lifestyle. But the question is, does everyone know how to manage and grow their money? The answer for that is, unfortunately, no. Nearly 78% of all Americans live pay check to pay check [1], and around 60% would not have the capabilities to pay a $1000 emergency expense [2]. It is appalling, isn't it? This is something that needs to be reversed, and that too fast! But what about the financially prudent folks who are smart enough to manage and invest their money? Do they look at all avenues for diversifying their investments? The answer to that is *nyet* as well.

People, upon receiving their income, often invest their money. This is done in broadly six asset classes – equities, bonds/fixed incomes, real estate, commodities, currencies, and alternative assets. All of them have different pros and cons, rates of returns, yields, etc… Still, they have one thing in common – money is invested so that people can grow their earnings over some time to spend liberally and save substantial amounts for their retirement. This leads to an inherent rush to identify the best investment options in the asset classes mentioned above.

The novel coronavirus pandemic has drawn many retail investors into investing (primarily in equities). Research shows that 15% of current retail investors entered the stock market in 2020 [3]. WOW, it is undoubtedly a huge number. But did investors show the same level of enthusiasm for other asset classes? Not really. Surely investments did pour into other asset classes, but the potential of growth of some of them is so high that they warrant a special discussion. So let's talk about a relatively untapped segment of alternative assets - Artwork Investing.

Artwork investing is when investors invest in fine art – usual paintings by famous artists. Since these are highly coveted, one expects their prices to appreciate over time. This is simply because when demand rises, more people are willing to buy that good for a higher amount, so the price increases.

Out of all retail investors, you would expect some to invest in artwork, some to just know about it, and others to know nothing about it, just because they simply couldn't care less – due to preconceived notions about it. One common notion in people's minds (including most adults I know of) is that artwork investing is just for High-Net-Worth individuals (HNI's).

When I was a young child, I was told that people have to be extremely rich, then go to an auction house full of other rich people, compete with them, and eventually outbid them to land a painting they like. Well, that is true even now. Ultra-rich people still use this procedure to obtain artwork that they like wholly. But, over the past decade, fractional investment in artwork has enhanced the ability of the public to buy expensive art that appeals to them. A young reader might think - *fractionally*? Oh, Lord! Mathematics everywhere. I get you. But trust me, it isn't that hard.

Fractional investing is when investors use the money they have to buy a fraction of a particular stock. Such a situation may arise when the price of a single share is so high on the market that one thinks they are better off buying a part (fraction) of that stock. If this still seems weird to you, imagine a $30,000 painting that you want to buy. That indeed is expensive! But, with the help of fractional investing, you can own a part of the painting, say $200! Isn't it convenient?

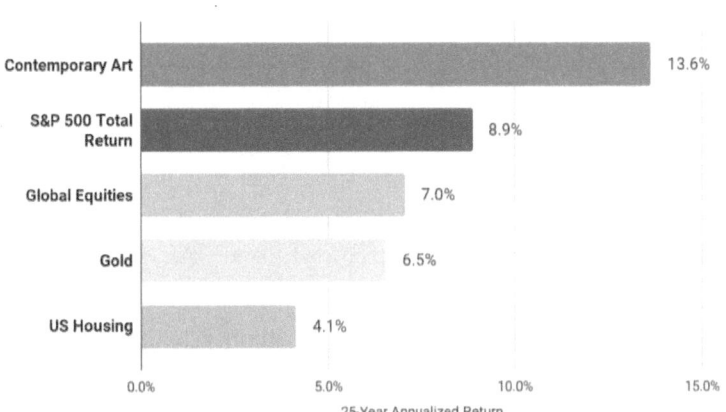

25-Year Annualized Performance
Contemporary Art Market [1] vs. Selected Asset Classes: 1995-2020 YTD[2]

Asset Class	25-Year Annualized Return
Contemporary Art	13.6%
S&P 500 Total Return	8.9%
Global Equities	7.0%
Gold	6.5%
US Housing	4.1%

Let's ponder about the financial economics of the artwork industry. This vertical bar chart by Masterworks [4] shows us the annualized performance of various asset categories. With a Compound Annual Growth Rate (CAGR) of 13.6%, the contemporary art market has the highest rate of return vis-a-vis other asset classes like gold, housing, and equities. An added advantage is that the art market typically gives better returns when interest rates are low [8].

This is because the art market is an inflationary hedge, and people flock towards it when inflation is high. If this sounds confusing, let's understand in layman terms. If hot chocolate fudge gives you seven utils (psychological units of satisfaction) and banoffee pie gives you ten utils, what would you choose? The latter option, right? Unless you're starving and want to eat both, of course! Essentially, the same is applicable in the world of financial markets. If the yield from one asset is low, naturally, you'll want to invest in another asset to get a higher yield.

Well, what is inflation? According to Investopedia, "Inflation is the decline of purchasing power of a given currency over time"[6]. What this means is that as time passes on, the value of money declines, with one of the main reasons being the excessive printing of notes by the central government. As they print more notes, there is more money circulating in the economy. Hence, consumers have more to spend, prices of scarce commodities rise, reducing the purchasing power of money for an individual.

One point to note is that the lockdown restrictions during the pandemic meant that there was not much footfall at art fairs and retail galleries. But the online sales of fine art boomed, showing a 4.7x increase [4]. Moreover, there was a surge in buyers, with 40% flocking to online auctions for the first time in 2020 [4]. This showed the growing popularity of this sector and its resilience during stressful times. Earlier, just rich people bought art. Now, with a rapidly globalizing and modernizing world, we have the technology to sell fractional shares of a painting, which automatically means that the middle-income class can buy it. This is a clear shift in cultural trend, as it makes investing in an alternative asset more equitable and inclusive.

10

VEGANISM & PLANT-BASED MEAT – A BRIGHT FUTURE?

Source of Image: [9], [10]

Mike owns a factory that generates harmful greenhouse gases by releasing life-threatening carbon emissions to bless the nearby villagers' lungs. Now, his son, Brent, goes to a school that teaches him the value of conserving the environment and instills a belief that wrongdoers should be punished.

Sure, Mike's seven-year-old will scold him for violating environmental norms, and he is probably going to take away just his hugging privileges for the night. But the law is not as lenient. It will penalize Mike. It will require Mike to pay a Carbon tax because his factory's activities adversely affect the environment. Who decides this tax amount? And the charge per unit of these emissions? Environment laws and costs...sounds like something related to environmental economics.

Environmental economics is a field that deduces and studies the economic and financial impact of environmental policies and actions. Studying this field has become very important because of the growing concerns of mistreatment of the environment. Where is this type of economics commonly applied? Let's discuss two widely growing derivatives of environmental economics - veganism and plant-based meat.

Part 1: Veganism

No meat. No pork. No bread. No eggs. No mayonnaise. NO HONEY. NOOO.

Of late, the world has seen a significant rise in people identifying themselves as vegan. According to United Nations estimates, that figure is estimated to be 79 million people, and the current world population is 7.9 billion [1]. 1% of the world population being vegan seems like a paltry number, doesn't it? Well, that figure is expected to grow exponentially over the next few years. The US has shown a 600% growth in 6 years from 2014-2020, and western countries such as the UK and Italy have also shown high growth [1]. Why is this happening though?

Considering the benefits of vegan food on health, research shows that people who eat vegan food are less likely to get certain kinds of cancer. Vegan food helps in reducing the risk of heart-related problems and helps in managing diabetes [5].

The environmental aspects reveal that the traditional meat industry is highly resource-intensive. This is proven by the fact that to produce one kilogram of beef, 25 kilograms of grain are needed to feed the animal, along with 15,000 litres of water. Other adverse side effects of the traditional meat industry include biodiversity loss, deforestation, land and water degradation. On the other hand, research has shown that plant-based industry produces at least ten times less greenhouse gas emissions than the traditional meat industry [7].

Part 2: Plant-Based Meats

Another category of environmentally beneficial foods is plant-based meats. Plant-based meat products are intended to look, smell and taste like meat but are made – entirely from plants and other non-animal products [4]. Some people call these impossible foods because their shape and taste are just like those of real meat!

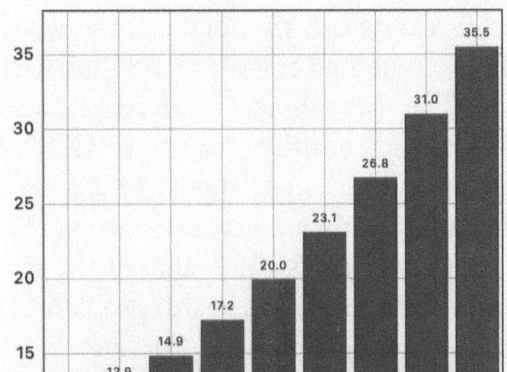

Market Value in billion U.S. dollars

The chart above [8] shows the forecasted market value of plant-based meat through 2027. The market value of plant-based meat in 2021 is 14.88 billion US dollars, and a projected market value in 2027 is 35.5 billion dollars. This is a Compounded Annual Growth Rate (CAGR) of 15.59 %. An ascending trend for demand is seen. And the reason for such growth is similar to that of the rise of veganism – primarily, both categories are environmentally sustainable and have certain health benefits. These two factors are bound to draw any environmentally and health-conscious individual!

Now let us talk about the economics of veganism and plant-based meat.

Environmental Economics

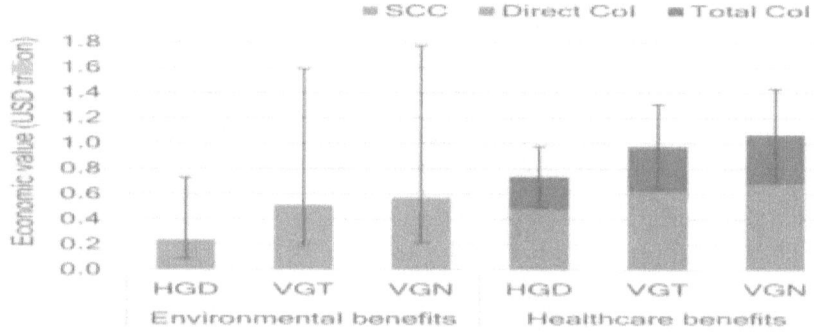

The above graph [11] by Proceedings of the National Academy of Sciences of the USA shows us the total economic value of different dietary preferences' combined environmental and healthcare benefits in trillion dollars. The three dietary preferences are Vegan (VGN), Vegetarian (VGT), and healthy eating (HGD). Environmental Benefits are derived using the social cost of carbon, and healthcare benefits are based on the estimated cost of illness [11]. Cost of illness is an economic term defined as the "value of the resources that are expended or forgone as a result of a health problem" [12]. It includes direct, indirect, and intangible costs. For instance, consider Kyle, who has leukaemia. He has a direct cost to pay which is the treatment and medical equipment cost. The lack of productivity due to the disease would be an indirect cost since he cannot monetize his forte. Meanwhile, the intangible cost he occurs is the fall in confidence and interest in certain aspects of life. These costs are weighing down on him from all directions and hampering his growth.

The social cost of carbon is the dollar estimate of the "economic damage that would result from emitting one ton of carbon dioxide into the atmosphere" [13]. A healthy eating diet (HGD), which contains meat and other non-vegetarian proteins, has a higher social cost of carbon due to using more natural resources for their production.

Clearly, in both environmental and healthcare benefits scenarios, the economic value of veganism is the highest, followed by vegetarianism and then healthy eating. You will be surprised to know that, as per research and calculations, close to 350 million additional people around the world can be fed if people in the US transition to a vegan diet [14]. *But what about the decline in GDP from the abandonment of meat-based industries?* Don't you think that people are selfish! Of course, it is to be thought about. The loss in economic GDP from reducing livestock meat production would be more than just offset by the rise of plant-based meat industries [14].

However, a point to be noted is that plant-based meat is undoubtedly more expensive than traditional meat. Why is that? The primary reason for that is the lower economies of scale of the companies making plant-based meat. Quick note, what do economies of scale mean? As we produce more and more goods on a large scale, the average total cost falls, so production becomes more efficient. This is a great way of earning profits compared to increasing prices, which might discourage consumers, especially in the case of elastic goods. To sum it up, economies of scale are the low costs of production achieved when the manufacturing/making of a product is done at a large scale [2]. Although gaining popularity of late, plant-based meat is still a fraction of the total animal livestock currently sold. Consumption, although growing, will take some time until it reaches optimal levels for the producers to reduce costs.

In the meantime, I feel that governments worldwide should encourage those deterred by the price of plant-based meat by giving subsidies for its purchase. If you haven't heard of subsidies, I will break it down for you. Subsidies are essential benefits provided to a certain sector for a specific purpose by making cash transfers or reducing taxes. They can be direct (reducing the amount directly) or indirect (changing other factors to achieve the goal) and are done keeping the public welfare in mind [3]. Other initiatives to encourage people to switch to plant-based meats shall include education on the health benefits of plant-based meats and the negative impact the traditional meat industry has on the environment.

11

QUINOA – THE NUTRITIONAL AND ECONOMIC VALUE

What's on a healthy plate? If you are looking for a high-fibre, gluten-free, protein-rich food, Quinoa is what you need!

Originated from South America, Quinoa has been the staple food for indigenous people of the Andean region for ages now. Bolivia and Peru together dominate the quinoa market, producing about 80% of Quinoa in the world, followed by Ecuador and the USA. Earlier, Quinoa was considered a mere common man's crop – it was cultivated primarily for self-consumption and sustenance and was considered as a "peasants' food with no commercial value [2].

However, this perception took a turn in the 1970s, when American and European consumers realized Quinoa's high nutritional values and saw it as an exotic and healthy superfood. The nutritional value this superfood possesses is quite phenomenal and is worth a try if one is in pursuit of a healthy diet. Consider a quick comparison: It surpasses even eggs when it comes to being rich in Fats, Iron and Proteins.

Table 1: Nutritional composition of quinoa compared with staple foods (%)

Components (%)	Quinoa	Meat	Eggs	Cheese	Cows milk	Human milk
Proteins	13.00	30.00	14.00	18.00	3.50	1.80
Fats	6.10	50.00	3.20		3.50	3.50
Carbohydrates	71.00					
Sugar					4.70	7.50
Iron	5.20	2.20	3.20		2.50	
Calories per 100 g	350	431	200	24	60	80

Source: FAO Regional Office for Latin America and the Caribbean, 2011. (Cited from Agrifood report, 2009 MDRT-BOLIVIA)

Source of Image: [1]

Since 2006, the demand for Quinoa started rising, and naturally, the prices soared since there was a grain shortage. So, when prices soared to such an extent, the farmers increased their output (supply) since they could earn higher profits. Of course, consumers were unhappy to pay thrice the amount they had to pay earlier to get the same amount of Quinoa, but the Bolivian and Peru farmers wanted to make more revenue, so they tried to sell more. The Quinoa no longer lay in the barn of a Bolivian farmer, ready for self-consumption. Instead, this food was out there in the markets for everyone to consume.

A concern that must be highlighted is that small producers compromised their own nutritional requirements and sought unhealthy alternatives such as pasta and bread in the bid to prosper by selling large quantities of quinoa produce for international markets. Within 2006 to 2011, quinoa consumption in Bolivia fell by 34% [3].

Ethical concerns regarding fair trade practices in the context of Quinoa have persisted. While large farmers gain direct monetary benefits from Quinoa trade, small farmers are not as successful as they are exploited at the hands of middlemen and do not necessarily have any means of accessing a better quality of life.

"The rich have become richer, and the poor have become poorer".

Wealthy Quinoa farmers have the requisite purchasing capacity to invest in high-quality machines that offer better returns to them, leaving the poorer ones to produce inefficient output as they use traditional methods.

Can you imagine what will happen when the craze about Quinoa ends when a new superfood comes into the picture?

Who will be at the greatest loss in case of this decline? South American farmers, of course. Why? Because a large population of these farmers earn their livelihood through the production of Quinoa. With a faint idea of what else they can produce to sustain themselves, these farmers will undoubtedly suffer huge losses. So many quinoa trade enthusiasts contend that consumers must buy these grains, given its ability to support an industry that reduces the burden of poverty. For instance, in 2011, in Bolivia, almost 40% of the rural population was living in poverty. However, as per S.-E. Jacobsen's study, the global trade of this precious crop was influential in alleviating poverty by sustaining rural farmers' livelihoods.

So, the government has to take the onus to ensure that South American farmers can cultivate an alternate crop food [3]. Moreover, research institutions need to study the climatic and geographical factors that can influence the growth of new crops. Another step to be taken by educational organizations and support groups would be to spread awareness amongst illiterate farmers about the alternative options available and how to optimise their present resources best.

The next time you walk into the supermarket, looking for a healthy snack, Quinoa is your go-to food! Remember, you're contributing to the economy with every purchase of the superfood you make.

12

YOGA – A STOREHOUSE OF HEALTH AND WEALTH

Source of Image: [6]

O *m. Shh, don't disturb me during my yoga routine Raj. Do you not know how good it is for my spine and soul?*

I hope you're not one of those people who are unaware of Yoga. If so, you need to wake up. Everyone - from your grandma to your biology professor - practices yoga because who doesn't like fitness? *I enter the chat**

Basically, Yoga is a spiritual discipline that involves meditating and maintaining specific body postures which are beneficial for the body and health. It is known to cure several ailments like diabetes, hypertension, certain liver problems, etc.

Known to have originated in Northern India about 5000 years ago, yoga has become one of our country's most significant cultural exports over the past few years. In fact, it has come a long way ever since. Some media reports indicate that the value of the yoga industry is about $88 billion worldwide. It turns out that in India, the value of the wellness industry has crossed $12 billion. According to statistics, there was an increase in the number of yoga practitioners in the US from 17 million in 2008 to 37 million by 2015. By 2025, if your mothers and grandmothers still show up in the coolest yoga pants, do keep in mind that they will be contributing enormously to the $215 billion global yoga industry[2]!

You often hear elders preaching discipline and calmness of mind in the direst situations. Guess what? Yoga can help you achieve both. Doing yoga is a cultural trend that offers long-term health benefits. The practice of this art instills in you a sense of power - of finding peace - even when your mind, body, and soul are trapped in chaos. Just as you follow a fixed routine in yoga, it also equips you with the ability to practice discipline in your daily life as you get fine-tuned to perform the same activities consistently.

It is considered so significant to a healthy lifestyle that the Prime Minister of India, Narendra Modi, recently launched the M-Yoga app in collaboration with WHO on International Yoga Day 2021. Moreover, many celebrities, such as Shilpa Shetty, David Beckham, Jennifer Aniston, Kate Hudson, etc., openly endorse yoga as an important mantra to stay fit [5]. Clearly, Yoga seems to be extremely valuable to all.

So why doesn't everyone practice yoga?

Are its benefits a myth, some might wonder. Others might have second thoughts about paying $15 for a Yoga Mat. Someone would rather stock Extra-Soft toilet paper. Hey, either way, genuinely keeping the soul clean! Where do I start...a home-based instructor? All of this seems just so expensive.

In reality, is it cheaper than the other forms of physical exercises you are familiar with? Maybe.

Let's talk about what all you purchase for different sports.

Interested in playing football? Football. Studs. Knee-length socks. A lot of open space. Probably join an academy if you really want to play professionally. How much would that cost?

A bomb.

Trying a hand at Basketball? What might you need? A basketball. Sports shoes. A synthetic jersey. A coach. And before you realize it, your feet have grown an inch longer, and your clothes have shrunk... so the whole spending cycle continues. Then you also want those fancy basketball shorts and a net to shoot the hoops at home. But we all know these items will be lying in the trunk till you forget about them. This phenomenon of over-consumption, driven by the purchase of an item or service, is known as Diderot's Effect [4]. It is like, *once you pop, you can't stop*. Yes, back to Pringles. But the difference is that apart from the classic Sour Cream & Onion flavour, you even want a cheesy dip that'll supplement your chips. And then a piece of candy to battle all that salt. You see, so much for one thing. How much would all that cost?

A bomb.

Let's talk about our all-time favourite, every teenager's pretentious hang out...you guessed it: the gym. Firstly, you need a membership which costs a sweet fee. A little too sweet, from anywhere ranging between *$250 to $900* [1]. *And of course, you need that stylish* gym wear which would not be less than *$20-25*.

In contrast, if you end up practicing yoga at home, you can simply wear your baggy, worn-out clothes. You don't need to spend huge bucks on hiring an instructor, as you can probably start with introductory YouTube videos. So, since Yoga is less costly than other forms of physical activities, would it not make sense to opt for it?

This is an underlying factor affecting demand. A change in the price of complementary goods would indirectly affect the demand for the good or service at hand. Complementary goods...what are those? It complements, i.e., is used with the given good, which is Yoga (service), and influences the demand for Yoga. If the price of the complementary good rises, your demand for the given good would naturally fall because, hey, this is too expensive for you to continue buying.

Here, a complementary good could perhaps be worn-out clothes. If they cost you almost nothing, you would not mind practicing yoga since you do not have to spend much on the entire yoga experience.

On the other hand, if we take the case of the entire football experience, the complementary good would be the football itself. Let's say, all of a sudden, the football starts costing more because Messi signed a deal with your football manufacturer, and as the brand value automatically increases, so does the price. Now, your football is pretty expensive, you might not want to buy it only and thus your demand for playing football, which is the entire football experience, falls.

Personally, if I were looking for a means of great physical exercise which was not at all costly, Yoga would be my top choice!

13

FIDGET SPINNERS

Source of Image: [5]

Remember the good ol' days when every toy shop was flooded with a myriad of fidget spinners? Catherine Hettinger is credited for inventing a fidget spinner in 1991. But what are they? How do they work, and what are they used for? Well, fidget spinners are palm-sized spinners consisting of a ball bearing that rests on a three-pronged plastic device. They can be flicked and spun around and are meant to be a fidgeting tool. What sparked interest in them was a YouTube video from 2017 featuring a bunch of teenagers performing crazy fidget spinner tricks. The low price, easy availability, and a wide choice of colours ensured that this toy found its way into a child's pocket - with millions of kids spending hours learning impressive tricks. This unisex toy, owing to its rapidly gaining widespread popularity, started affecting classroom discipline. Children used to compare their spinners during classes, consequently disturbing the classroom decorum. As a result, many schools in the UK and US banned them - meaning all the hours students had spent on learning impressive tricks went down the drain.

Initially, the inventor of this delightful toy secured a patent on the fidget spinners for many years but had to yield in 2005 as she could not pay her renewal fee [1]. Now, since there was no patent required, fidget spinners' suppliers jumped at the opportunity to increase their supply to earn quick profits. Chinese companies that manufactured gadget accessories saw the fidget spinner sector as a profitable avenue and produced fidget spinners in bulk quantities, thereby increasing their profits. Now, anyone could produce them and control their prices. The massive supply brought the prices down from about $100 to $4. Mom and pop shops worldwide were able to buy these unpatented and non-branded goods at cheap prices.

In a few months, the number of fidget spinner sellers rose to 8000, with an inventory of 600,000 such spinners. By May 2017, their global demand skyrocketed. The fidget spinner frenzy also resulted in a digital buzz for its app, which topped the downloads charts.

What's so interesting about the fidget spinner fad is that consumers - in this case, children - randomly discovered them and they exploded in popularity due to social media.

Consider another reason for the success of this object: the big box toy retailers did not have the power to manipulate the sales of this product. Chinese suppliers seized the opportunity of the rise in demand for this product and directly tied up with e-retailers like Amazon and Alibaba to offer it to the crowds. Thus, rather than involving wholesalers or any middlemen, these suppliers directly reached out to consumers. This logic of disintermediation - connecting consumers directly with manufacturers without additional distribution channels - rests on the idea that middlemen are often the source of inefficiency as they might indulge in unethical methods to secure higher profits [2]. Furthermore, it implies that the direct linkage of a manufacturer to the final consumer might help in reducing logistics costs.

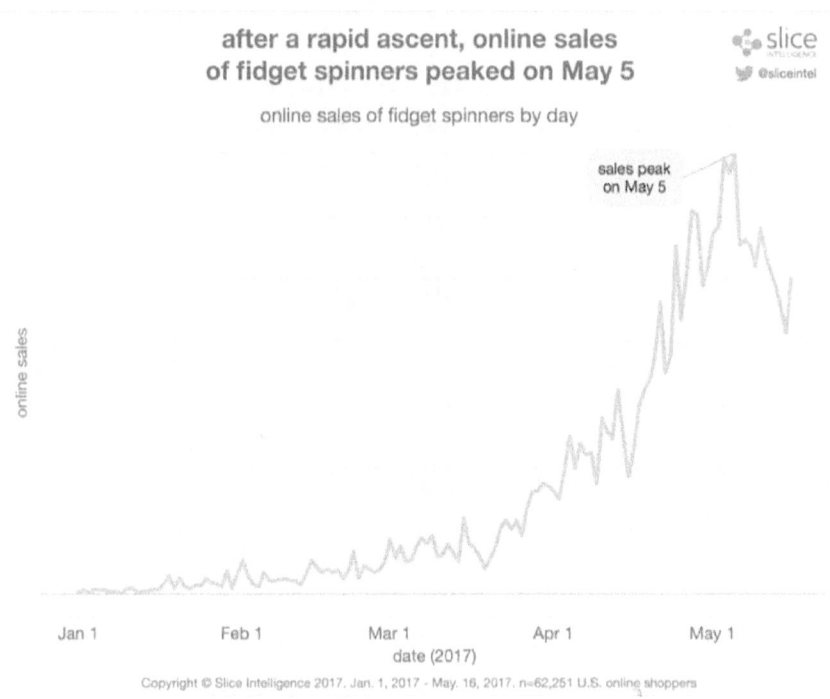

While it certainly helped small suppliers, it also made them realize that middlemen are essential for launching a new product in the market. They help in converting a fad or a trend into a viable and sustainable business [2]. Middlemen are responsible for a plethora of tasks that might not be the forte of a manufacturer. For instance, apart from manufacturing the product, a toy company has several functions it must focus on Marketing - ascertaining the feasibility of the 4 Ps i.e. Product, Price, Place, and Promotion, Intellectual Property Rights, distribution strategies, and knowledge on when to stop manufacturing a certain product. All these additional areas require the expertise and guidance of this vital channel partner, middlemen.

Similar to most cases of products that are bolstered by a fad, these small pocket-sized spinners reached the sky but fell hard on the ground after reaching their saturation point, which was in 2017 [3].

However, circa 2021, this product has spun its way to the top yet again, but with even more force: the sales have exceeded the numbers clocked in the first round of the fidget-spinner craze. The new fidget toy market has "diversified its scope of products to include tangles, marble mesh, silicone poppers, and squishy balls."

A major contributor to their resurgence has been the social app TikTok, which can showcase multiple fast-paced videos covering wide, rare interests. Just a single search for "fidget toys" reveals countless videos people have made as part of the fidget toy 'trend'.

Today, there exists a symbiotic relationship between TikTok and Fidget toys. People promoting this toy simply need quick fingers and fun tricks to attract the youth [4]. Moreover, these fidget spinners might even act as a tool to improve concentration amongst children, which is significant during the COVID-19 situation that burdens them with anxiety and boredom. Let's see if this current resurgence in the popularity of fidget toys can sustain a bit longer than the first one!

14

Sony Walkman – Former Running Champion

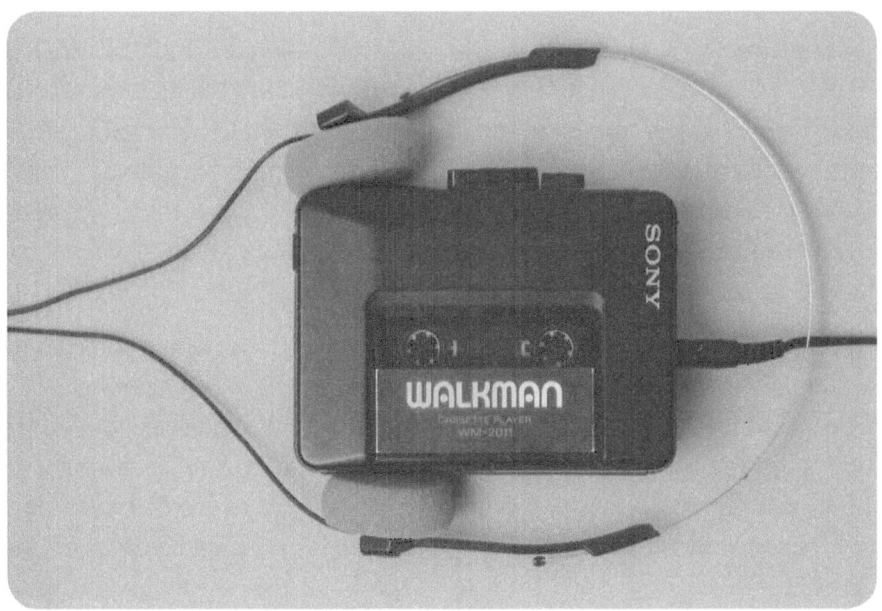

Source of Image: [8]

July 1, 1979. The day that the Sony Walkman TPS-L2 was unveiled. A mere rectangular box of blue and silver metal, with tiny buttons, attached to headphones, the Walkman was a transformational step towards communications in those times [1].

Acting as headphones, the Walkman was a portable set that allowed anyone listening to unpopular music to keep it private. In fact, it was the invention that brought to light that portable yet private usage of audio was possible.

It wasn't a surprise that in Japan, more than 30,000 units of Walkman were sold at a hefty price of $200 each, and that too within two months of the launch of the product [2].

Soon in 1983, seeing the success of this device, the Walkman II or WM-20 model was launched, which now was as big as the cassette case. There was a huge craze for this device in the 80s. Catering to the preferences of a broad class of individuals - ranging from high school students listening to the coolest pop-tunes to a retiree listening to soft countryside music - the Walkman successfully engaged all demographics! [3]

It is a well-known fact that effectively piquing the target audience's interest is a goal that is crucial in the nascent stages of a product's launch. Thus, to achieve this, the Walkman was advertised through huge marketing campaigns that intrigued the sentiments of the youth about concepts relating to mobility, a sense of belonging, and the freedom provided by music. It emphasized that the characteristics of a trendy person - young, active, vigorous, and cool - were only associated with the Walkman. What a perfect strategy! This association boosted the success of Sony's subsequent product lines, including the PlayStation and its digital camera [4].

For sustaining in the dynamic environment while holding the leading position in the public's eye, the Walkman had to evolve constantly. Enter the CD Walkman, or you can say" the Discman." Given the existing surge in craze for CDs in the 90s, the CD Walkman seized this market opportunity and was widely preferred by the youth.

The Walkman was a vital contributor to Sony's success and annual revenue of about $60 billion. Starting from the first video cassette recorder in 1971, the Walkman personal stereo in 1979, the CD in 1982, MD in 1992, and PlayStation game in 1995 till the Network Walkman digital music player in 1999, and many more innovations helped build Sony's brand value and market capitalization that rests at $137.3 billion today [6].

While you might think that oh, what is the big deal about Walkman? Sure, it was a technological advancement towards communication, but what's the buzz about? Consider how Walkman influenced culture [5]. Compared to the past, where audios would have to be confined to Television and Radio, the Walkman could reach a wider audience beyond the boundaries of home.

Often, it is believed that the innovation of Walkman impacted the interactions between humans and technology. The revelation of the Walkman as a successful commercially viable product paved the way for a wide array of hi-fi products - personal devices like mobile phones, laptops, and tablets were the subsequent innovations that were successful after gauging the consumer reactions and apprehensions to the portability of devices.

People always enjoy the ability to exercise control over their belongings, which in my opinion, was an added advantage of the Walkman. While the radios would play only certain channels at specified times, which was often unpleasant, Walkman users could get lost in their own world of music, controlled at their discretion [3]. In the 80s and the 90s, the Walkman was the most popular device for individuals to listen to music and sold just under 200 million units during its lifespan.

However, the release of Apple's iPod in 2001 led to Sony Walkman's sales declining considerably. The iPod was economically convenient for consumers as they could directly purchase music from the comforts of their homes, rather than frequently visiting stores and spending on buying cassettes. These factors undoubtedly contributed to the iPod's success. However, the Sony Walkman was impacted by this change in trend. At this point, cassettes became almost obsolete [7].

They say that the originals always hold the charm, which was aptly seen in the case of Sony's unsuccessful attempts to digitize the Walkman. Despite the latest touch screen model and wifi facilities, the late 90s' youth was not as passionate about the Walkman anymore [1]. Even though Sony offers a variety of highly distinguished Walkman models today, the millennial population will continue to picture this device as the elegant silver and blue cassette player of the 80s decade [4].

15

MINK FUR – ETHICS VS ECONOMICS

Source of Image: [5]

Gucci bags. Ferrari. Designer Wear. What comes to your mind when you first hear about these? If you belong to a middle income or working class, you would call these luxury items. Why call this luxury and not a regular good? Well, for someone who earns in the median income bracket, luxury is defined as "indulgence and pleasure of wealthy, pleasant, and sumptuous life; something that is considered an indulgence and not a necessity" [6].

As per Abraham Maslow, all beings are motivated by needs. The hierarchy below illustrates that we tend to satisfy the most critical needs, those relating to survival. Gradually, when the primary level needs get sorted, we start fulfilling our high order needs. For instance, Initially, animal fur was a necessity for warmth. Now, this fur is a luxury item that denotes status and prestige, a component satisfying a higher level of needs - esteem needs. [1]

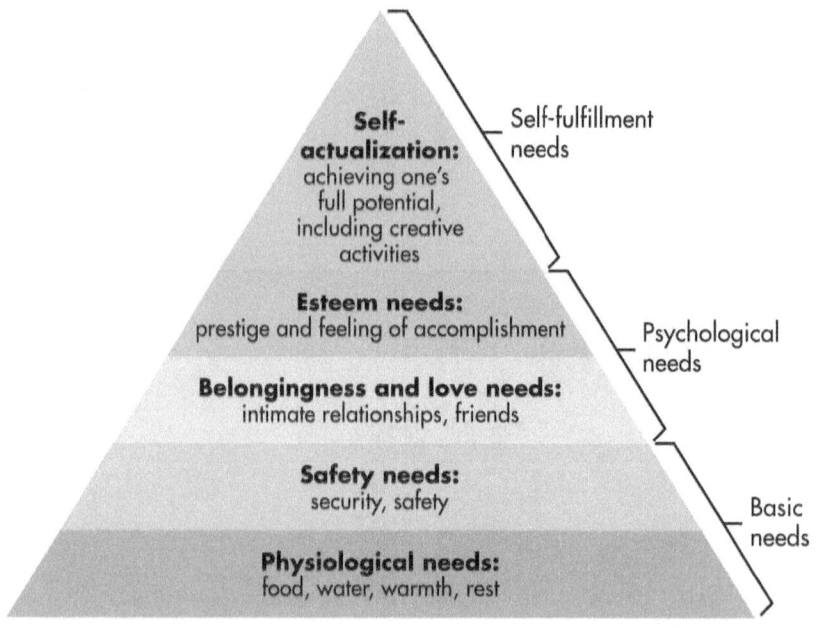

Over several decades, fur has maintained itself as a noble and commercially significant item. Mink fur, in particular, has captured the international market. Majorly, the suppliers are the United States, Canada, and the Scandinavian countries. With the help of effective scientific breeding methods and other high-end procedures, producers have mastered producing the highest quality of mink fur possible. Proponents of mink fur usage, especially the members of the fur trade, emphasize the fact that mink fur is sustainable. Moreover, it helps in supporting about 117,000 small-scale enterprises and one million individuals that engage in the global mink fur industry, which has a turnover of ₹3 trillion ($40 billion) [1] [7].

Primitive people initially used fur to protect themselves against harsh climatic conditions. So, from the point of view of a hunter-gatherer, rudimentary fur coats would be a necessity. Sounds like a new term? Let me define it for you. Just as the name suggests, necessity goods are those which you need for survival. The demand for them is relatively inelastic. *"Don' spring new words on me."*

No vague term goes unexplained. Let me define it for you! Inelastic means that it is not very flexible. In other words, it is not easy to change the demand to a large extent. Even if the price fluctuates (rises), one cannot expect the demand for a necessity to change a lot, whatever the price may be. Because to sustain, you have to pay it! In this sense, since the demand for fur was inelastic for primitive people, they were unlikely to change their demand for it by a large extent.

However, now times have changed. Fur is no longer a necessity thanks to our centralized heating systems and, of course, global warming. If you're found wearing a thick mink fur coat in the streets of New York, you are probably rich. Now, mink fur has earned the title of a luxury good. The demand for luxury goods is elastic. The logic is pretty much the opposite. When expensive goods, which we do not require in our day-to-day lives, become even more costly since the price rises, we are likely to forgo our demand for that particular good. For instance, I am saving up money to buy an exclusive Chanel perfume costing Rs 1,00,000. Now, all of a sudden, the company decides to raise the price of this perfume to Rs 1,50,000. Woah! That is quite a hefty increase. I might as well use this money somewhere else. I am no longer willing to pay such a huge sum, and the demand for this Chanel perfume falls collectively this way.

Nevertheless, you must keep in mind that there are exceptions to this principle as well. The law of demand can be violated, and thus luxury goods might not always be elastic. Ever heard of Veblen goods? Such types of goods see a direct relationship with price. As price rises, the demand does too. Why is that? Well, Veblen goods have a factor of social prestige attached to them. It makes people feel like they have an edge over others simply by possessing a particular good. For instance, exclusive art or cars and precious stone would fall in this category. Fur now occupies a similar status in the luxury market.

Being a novelty, mink fur consistently sees rapid price hikes. Some theories suggest that a resemblance can be observed between the fur's market craze and a bubble - neither can last indefinitely. The outcome of this burst will mean a sharp decline in its price, though by what volume? We'll have to wait and see.

In fact, due to Covid-19, the mink fur industry has been hit hard as many livestock farms have been decimated. Moreover, some Western countries advocate strict anti-fur policies. Denmark - a leading supplier of mink fur - engaged in massive culling of mink farms in November 2020, as concerns regarding the virus from livestock surfaced. On the other hand, China, enjoying the status of the second largest supplier of mink fur, saw this as an opportunity to continue hiking the prices given the limited supply of mink fur. [2]

A major pitfall in the mink fur industry is the pricey mink fur coats, which are very much *er, so to speak*...made from animals. Suppliers ought to consider the loss of life of this precious animal which is tortured and isolated in inhabitable conditions, which indirectly leads to its death unless killed directly.

Animal rights activists are raising concerns about this issue more than ever before. They contend that using steel-jaw traps and electrocution of these animals is unethical. Since the late twentieth century, organizations like People for the Ethical Treatment of Animals (PETA) have been passionately involved in conquering this battle against animal abuse by waging heavy anti-fur campaigns.

Almost 17 years ago, in 2004, PETA director Dawn Carr contended that animals should never be forced to bear the brunt as fashion victims. Furthermore, she called out that synthetic fur should be used in contemporary times, given its visual and physical resemblance to real mink fur [3]. Hey, imagine what if synthetic fur completely replaces mink fur. As consumer tastes shift towards such a type of ethical fashion practice, the demand for these artificial fibers will rise while causing a decline in demand for mink fur.

However, many ardent supporters of this mink fur industry have a counter-argument to using synthetic furs: its contribution to depletion of non-renewable resources. Acrylic is often used to make these synthetic fibres that replicate fur. In the process, they contribute to unsustainable practices. Compared to mink fur, which is biodegradable, these fibres take millions of years to decompose in the environment. In context to this issue, they argue that such artificial fibres are harmful to biodiversity in the long run [4].

Being a supporter of ethical fashion, I would still opt for apparel that uses the latest technologies to develop products cloning animals' treasured components. To date, the public's opinion on the usage of mink fur in the fashion industry remains divided: *is it acceptable to forgo the environment to save minks?* Sustainable alternatives to real fur seem like the only common ground that can satisfy everyone.

16

SUSTAINABLE FASHION – A NEW ECO-FRIENDLY ALTERNATIVE

Source of Image: [4]

"**I** wore that dress last time, Mom, not again!"

"Ugh. Okay Tia, what about this orange one? It's been 2 years, my $80 is rotting away under a heap of clothes in your dusty closet, which you never bother clearing out!"

"Mom, Aisha wore the same one in a jute texture to the mall last week. Do you want to embarrass me by making me wear something that looks like a copy of her dress?"

"I'm not spending my hard-earned money only to hear you throw a fit about clothes. Do you realize how many resources you're wasting?"

"What' *resources*'? It's just money that we're talking about."

Uh Oh.

Enter the world of oblivion. What are these resources that are being wasted? Let's chalk them out for Tia. She is an unreasonable teenager and represents many peers who choose to remain fixated on buying new clothes without actually considering their costs and environmental implications. But we will conquer this first step of awareness.

Firstly, what Tia must consider are the costs that her parents bear. She must value the money they spend on her. Also, Tia has to look at the environmental damage that is caused due to her irrational and impulsive purchases of apparel. A report by UNEP and the Ellen McArthur Foundation highlights that the fashion industry contributes 10% to annual global carbon emissions. Furthermore, the industry's greenhouse emissions might even surge beyond 50% by 2030. This is alarming. With the rise in demand for apparel, global figures for clothes will rise from 62 million metric tons in 2019 to 102 million in the next decade. The unsustainable usage of plastic during the packaging process further aggravates plastic pollution caused by brands. What's more, this industry also consumes 93 billion metric cubic meters of water each year, which alone could meet the water consumption needs of 5 million people [1].

Thankfully, many people like Aisha have woken up to the perils posed by unsustainable fashion. She firmly believes that fast fashion, which is inspired by trends and requires high levels of resource and energy investment for quick manufacturing processes [3], is detrimental to the environment. They are sold to gullible consumers at affordable prices and promised quality, and are frequently made available. What ends up happening is that consumers get attracted to these trendy clothes and purchase them to show them off. As a result, their peers also try to match their level and purchase fast fashion products. This herd behaviour ultimately leads to massive consumption, and the sad fact is that people also start discarding more clothes, which might not be biodegradable. The report further indicates that the average person today buys about 60% more clothing now than they did in the early 2000s. Only less than 1% of this used clothing is recycled into new garments [1]. This is partly because it is made from highly non-biodegradable (synthetic fibers), and partly because people just don't bother to recycle their clothes due to lack of awareness and logistical complexities. Tia and her ilk contribute $500 billion in lost value due to discarding, underutilization, and low rates of recycling used apparel [1].

So, the second step in this quest for sustainable fashion would be observing and adopting practices followed by Aisha and consumers like her. She first clears her wardrobe to see whether she *needs* those extra pairs of baggy pants. If yes, she opts for those brands that focus on a sustainable approach. These brands should use biodegradable textiles. No animals should be harmed during the process of manufacturing. For instance, instead of using real crocodile skin, brands should look for realistic alternative textiles. Aisha also considers whether the company pays its workers fairly. Child labour is a big no-no. She highly recommends buying from brands that constantly innovate and sell apparel that can be recycled easily and draw their resources from mother nature so that they exist in abundance even in the future.

Thrift culture is another upcoming fad that 'environmentally conscious' consumers are leaning towards. How this industry works is that people sell their "pre-loved" or unused items to those individuals who might be willing to buy them. Thus, in a way, this promotes the reusing cycle and also allows sellers to make a tiny profit. The energy used up in processing clothes is avoided, and resources are not wasted. Moreover, thrift stores are instrumental in strengthening communities and help in providing support to small businesses. Unlike setting up a store in a market that requires land, labour, and capital - components that are hard to acquire easily, a thrift store can be set up without much hassle.

Nowadays, people have adapted to an online mode of thrifting owing to the COVID-19 pandemic norms. Thus, it is cost and time-effective, as the entrepreneur just has to make provisions for delivering the apparel to the consumer, and payments can be made via credit card or cash. Warehousing is also not an issue since a minimum duration of dispatch and arrival is established. While you might think that a thrifting culture does not contribute to the economy, you must consider how it has led to a rise in employment opportunities for ancillary services now [2]. As the income of people rises, so does the demand for luxurious or branded goods, but this is a practice that isn't necessarily environmentally conscious. For the sake of the well-being of our environment, I wouldn't mind buying a gorgeous dress that has been worn just once, even if I can afford more.

So, hopefully, Tia learned a lot about how the battle for sustainability has entered the field of fashion and its perception in today's time. All Aisha would say is to remember to make the right choices as a rational consumer. Keep working to take it a notch higher with sustainable fashion!

17

WOMEN EMPOWERMENT: CHANGING SOCIAL TREND

Source of Image: [2]

The rise in social, political, and economic inequalities between men and women and amongst women themselves, due to disparities, is a sad reality of our country.

Previously, the mindset of the Indian patriarchal society was oppressive towards women as a large number of women were engaged as homemakers. There are many factors why economic and social opportunities were denied to them: social stigma about working outside the familial dominion, societal pressures about tending to "motherly" duties, vulnerabilities due to lack of financial dependence, illiteracy, and historical norms.

However, since the 1990s, the emergence of women in all types of professional and personal domains can be observed. More and more women are independent in terms of financial resources, job opportunities, and leadership roles in the workplace and family life. You may wonder what caused this massive change in the rigid orthodox system? Such a change in social trends can be attributed to a change in women's perspective about themselves and their struggles and movements for liberation. Many government schemes are constantly laid out to aid women to gain access to an equitable distribution of resources, and society at large has become conscious of the equal position of women in society.

Women's progress, especially in the past 25 years has led to the emergence of various products and facilities, catering to the rising demands owing to increased workforce participation in India.

Since women now have to go outside and earn a livelihood, they can no longer devote much time to house chores. Activities like cooking, cleaning, taking care of children, etc., have to be handled by opting for alternatives. They have adopted a different lifestyle to sustain the various personal and professional roles in life. Let's analyse a few key components of the economy that women's economic growth has influenced.

+ **A rise in demand for fast-moving consumer goods -** The increase in consumption of packaged food, beverages, toiletries, and other essential goods has given rise to the increased demand for these items.

◆ **Rise in demand for durable goods** - In contrast to the past, where women would perform the household cleaning tasks manually, they now rely on devices that can reduce their time, effort, and labour. Thus, home appliances like vacuum cleaners and automated cleaners are utilized. Moreover, other electrical appliances such as refrigerators, microwaves, and mixers have seen a rise in demand as cooking no longer entails spending the entire day over a stove and trying to serve fresh food. Women often prefer cooking a meal and storing it overnight in the refrigerator for later use.

◆ **Rise in demand for crèches:** Because married women cannot work in a professional environment from home (although the COVID-19 pandemic may make it a long-term way of life), they often face issues relating to child care. With these changing social trends combined with urbanization and migration, the joint family system is impacted severely, so garnering their support for childcare is not always practical. Unable to overlook the basic daily activities of the child, a mother may opt for a crèche to provide better, focussed care in her absence.

◆ **Rise in demand for luxury items:** The contribution of women to the economy is personally quite rewarding for them because now, they have more disposable income to spend on leisurely goods and services for themselves. Therefore, the demand for personal care, make-up, designer apparel, bags, and shoes has risen. On the other hand, those goods which were earlier purchased out of necessity or a budget constraint, see a decline in such scenarios. The two types of goods indicated above are referred to as **normal** and **inferior goods** in economic terms. The income elasticity of demand implies that as there is a change in the level of income, there is a change in the demand for different categories of goods, as mentioned above. With higher levels of income, the demand for normal goods rises. Whereas, with a fall in income, the demand for inferior goods rises.

Another quick example would be a mobile phone. Let's say you own a particular model which is decent but not as cool as the expensive one you've desired for so long. Suddenly, all your hard work pays off, and you earn a bonus! Now, you might get the sudden urge to treat yourself to that pricey phone. This is a normal good for you. On the other hand, consider the scenario where you go bankrupt or bear major losses. You really cannot afford such high-end products. You may even consider shifting to a cheaper, more mediocre type of phone. This would be an inferior good since with the fall in income, you are forced to buy "inferior" goods.

Source of Image: [3]

♦ **Changes in Women's formal wear industry:** The spiralling effect of this change in social trend has also influenced the marketing and shopping experiences. In the past few decades, the fashion industry has transitioned from manufacturing and stitching formal wear (shirts, pants, coats) for just men to increased production and variety for women. Promoting neutrality of formal wear while introducing blouses, skirts, and dresses have been a large number of brands' approach.

A sustainable apparel brand, Venn, has a vision of catering to the fashion needs based on lifestyle choices of women in all domains - personal and professional. The brand's founder, Pooja Khanna, pointed out how the Indian women formal wear market crossed $460 billion in 2017. Furthermore, this industry was anticipated to grow at a CAGR of 6% in the 2017-2024 period, reaching a revenue of $690 billion by 2024. [1]

Finally, I would conclude by emphasizing the fact that the socio-economic progress of India has been accelerated by the changing trends of employment opportunities available to women. Having an influx of women in the STEM fields and corporate world is eventually beneficial for our country's GDP. While we are already on the path to future development, we must ensure human resource development, especially of women, to optimize human capital for the best productivity. The best way to do so would be through training programs, educational opportunities, and facilitating more participation of women in decision-making and leadership roles in the professional world.

Words Often Associated with "Fad"

Nine days' wonder

Someone or something that fosters a short-lived sensation [5]

Cult

A group of people showing intense devotion to a cause, person, or work (as a film) [5]

Caprice

A sudden impulsive and apparently unmotivated idea or action [5]

Dernier cri

A practice or interest that is very popular for a short time [5]

Whim

A sudden impulsive and apparently unmotivated idea or action [5]

Vogue

A fashion or general liking, especially one that is temporary [2]

Dandyism

Excessive concern with matters of dress; foppishness [3]

Energumen

A wild enthusiast; a faddist [4]

Faddism

An inclination for adopting fads [6]

Mania

A manifestation of intense enthusiasm for something; craze or fad, as musicomania

Characteristics of a Fad

- Fads are perpetuated by an emotional need to purchase and are based on the hype created in social surroundings and on idealistic product perceptions.

- The benefits of a particular fad are often misleading and do not satisfy the consumers in the manner anticipated. Thus they offer low utility to consumers at times.

- They see a boom and a bust, i.e., a sharp rise in followers and an almost equal decline in interest, eventually.

- Many times, a single brand's product or service becomes appealing to the extent of a fad. It has a narrow consumer segment.

- Often, just after we purchase a particular item, it loses its value in terms of satisfaction provided. Thus the fad no longer seems exciting.

Words Often Associated with Trends

Lean

To bend or deviate from an upright position; stand at a slant; incline. [1]

Predilection

Condition of favouring or liking; tendency towards; proclivity; predisposition. [1]

Movement

A tendency or trend in some particular sphere of activity. [1]

Inclination

Any action, practice, or thing, toward which one is inclined. [1]

Tendency

Movement or prevailing movement in a given direction. [2]

Craze

A strong habitual desire or fancy; a crotchet. [1]

Propensity

A tendency, preference, or attraction. [1]

Furore

A great, widespread outburst of admiration or enthusiasm; craze; rage. [1]

Penchant

A strong liking or fondness; inclination; taste. [1]

Proclivity

A natural or habitual tendency or inclination, esp. toward something discreditable. [1]

BIBLIOGRAPHY

What are fads?

1. 29-What-are-the-four-categories-of-fads-Object-Fads-are-items-that-people

2. https://www.encyclopedia.com/social-sciences-and-law/economics-business-and-labor/businesses-and-occupations/fads

What are Trends?

1. https://dictionary.cambridge.org/us/dictionary/english/trend

2. https://www.linkedin.com/pulse/how-can-you-differentiate-trends-from-fads-make-them-meabh-quoirin/

3. https://www.designpoolpatterns.com/do-you-know-the-difference-between-trend-fad/

4. https://www.inc.com/jeffrey-phillips/are-you-chasing-a-fad-or-a-trend.html

5. https://specialties.bayt.com/en/specialties/q/286314/explain-the-difference-between-trend-and-fad/

6. https://globaltrendspotter.wordpress.com/2017/03/24/categorizing-trends-what-are-the-different-types-of-trends/

7. https://www.jisc.ac.uk/guides/vision-and-strategy-toolkit/trends-analysis

Economics and Cultural Behaviour

1. Photo by Chris Briggs on Unsplash
2. Photo by Sydney Rae on Unsplash

3. https://www.ecnmy.org/learn/you/social-influences-culture-information/

4. https://mpra.ub.uni-muenchen.de/69747/1/MPRA_paper_69747.pdf

5. https://www.hec.edu/en/knowledge/articles/culture-and-economy-understanding-dynamics-globalization

Chapter 1: Tulip's Bubble

1. https://www.moneyunder30.com/economic-bubbles

2. https://www.atlasobscura.com/articles/the-most-beautiful-tulip-in-history-cost-as-much-as-a-house

3. https://www.fluwel.com/eating-tulip-bulbs

Chapter 2: Instagram Reels – The next Indian Tiktok

1. https://timesofindia.indiatimes.com/business/india-business/the-ban-impact-tiktoks-parent-company-may-lose-6-billion/articleshow/76756985.cms

2. https://blog.hootsuite.com/instagram-demographics/

3. https://influencermarketinghub.com/instagram-reels-stats/

4. https://www.freelanceinformer.com/creative-editorial-media/brand-influencers-to-unionise-in-the-uk-and-us-as-influencer-industry-set-to-grow-to-15bn-by-2022/

5. http://economicstudents.com/2020/03/the-economics-behind-becoming-an-instagram-influencer/

6. https://www.livemint.com/news/india/virat-kohli-highest-paid-indian-on-instagram-after-overtaking-this-celebrity-11625230299378.html

7. https://www.scoopwhoop.com/How-Much-Instagrammers-Get-Paid-For-One-Post/

8. https://www.thehindu.com/life-and-style/fashion/dance-marketing-saris-sari-sarees-instagram-reels-video-video-

clips-the-hindu-weekend-traditional-wear-young-women-choregraphy-dance-steps-dance-moves-sales-purchase-buy/article34394031.ece

9. https://slate.com/technology/2020/08/tiktok-india-ban-china.html

Chapter 3: Memeonomics

1. https://www.axios.com/meme-economy-tesla-elon-musk-c1e9c225-d8e2-4953-a591- 0a29dacf2d4a.html

2. https://inomics.com/advice/top-memes-all-economists-will-love-1305239

3. https://www.reddit.com/r/memes/comments/cqgqt0/meme_economics/

4. https://www.pinterest.com/pin/715368722043791663/

5. https://imgflip.com/i/4rw3zw

6. https://www.lexico.com/definition/meme

7. https://www.econlib.org/library/Enc/OpportunityCost.html

8. https://timesofindia.indiatimes.com/life-style/spotlight/the-demand-of-meme-makers-in-the-industry/articleshow/74907892.cms

9. https://www.thedrum.com/news/2017/03/22/gucci-takes-dip-the-ever-dangerous-world-memes-promote-its-watches

10. https://www.complex.com/pop-culture/2019/04/nickelodeon-releases-official-spongebob-meme-figures

Chapter 4: Podcast – A future broadcast?

1. https://www.inc.com/tanya-hall/5-reasons-it-might-be-time-to-start-a-podcast.html

2. https://www.statista.com/chart/22184/change-in-podcast-listeners-audience-project/

3. https://www.lexico.com/definition/podcast

4. https://www.elegantthemes.com/blog/marketing/what-is-a-podcast-a-brief-historyhow-to-listen-to-them-and-how-to-create-them

5. https://www.campaignlive.co.uk/article/why-podcasting-perfect-advertising-times uncertainty/1701577

6. https://techcrunch.com/2019/08/21/after-a-breakout-year-looking-ahead-to-the-future-of-podcasting/

7. https://www.edisonresearch.com/infinite-dial-2019/

8. http://blog.bloomads.com/blog/the-benefits-of-podcast-marketing-tips-to-get-started

9. https://www.bloomberg.com/news/articles/2021-06-29/amazon-acquires-smartless podcast-for-as-much-as-80-million

Chapter 5: OTT – Are viewers chilling?

1. https://www.financialexpress.com/brandwagon/ad-revenues-digital-ott-stealing-the-show-televisions-channels-losing-appeal/2113735/

2. https://www.bbc.com/news/business-52376022

3. Photo by Nicolas J Leclercq on Unsplash

4. https://economictimes.indiatimes.com/industry/media/entertainment/indian-ott-market-has-a-potential-to-reach-5bn-by-2023-bcg/articleshow/66709416.cms?from=mdr

Chapter 6: Subscription Boxes – Anytime, anywhere…

1. https://just4ubox.com/what-is-a-subscription-box/

2. https://pitchbook.com/news/articles/the-science-and-data-behind-the-subscription-box craze

3. https://www.linkedin.com/pulse/economics-subscription-based-revenue-model-part-1- scott-gilbert/

4. https://www.globalbrandsmagazine.com/the-pros-and-cons-of-monthly-subscription boxes/

5. https://searchdatamanagement.techtarget.com/definition/big-data

6. https://www.askmen.com/entertainment/guy_gear/the-best-shaving-subscription boxes-for-father-s-day.html

7. https://www.forbes.com/sites/andriacheng/2018/05/30/the-subscription-box-industryis-getting-more-crowded-than-ever/?sh=7c607c6c3a39

8. https://www.mckinsey.com/industries/technology-media-and-telecommunications/ourinsights/thinking-inside-the-subscription-box-new-research-on-ecommerce-consumers

Chapter 7: The craze behind NFTs

1. https://techcrunch.com/2017/12/03/people-have-spent-over-1m-buying-virtual-cats-on-the-ethereum-blockchain/

2. https://www.prnewswire.com/news-releases/snoop-dogg-announces-the-release-of-his-first-nft-collection-a-journey-with-the-dogg-301259014.html

3. https://moneyweek.com/investments/alternative-finance/bitcoin/602928/what-are-nfts-and-why-are-they-so-popular

4. https://www.nytimes.com/2021/03/30/arts/design/nft-bubble.html

5. https://www.forbes.com/advisor/investing/nft-non-fungible-token/

Chapter 8: Bitcoin – An asset class or a medium of exchange?

1. https://en.wikipedia.org/wiki/Bitcoin

2. https://www.coindesk.com/price/bitcoin

3. https://www.reuters.com/technology/chinese-financial-payment-bodies-barred cryptocurrency-business-2021-05-18/

4. https://www.cnbc.com/2021/06/05/el-salvador-becomes-the-first-country-to-adopt bitcoin-as-legal-tender-.html

5. https://www.bbc.com/news/business-57507386

6. https://www.hindustantimes.com/trending/220-million-worth-of-bitcoin-locked-away-as-man-forgets-password-101611025805874.html

Chapter 9: Artwork Investing: The new money making proposition

1. https://www.cnbc.com/2019/01/09/shutdown-highlights-that-4-in-5-us-workers-live paycheck-to-paycheck.html

2. https://www.cnbc.com/2019/01/23/most-americans-dont-have-the-savings-to-cover-a 1000-emergency.html

3. https://www.cnbc.com/2021/04/08/a-large-chunk-of-the-retail-investing-crowd-gottheir-start-during-the-pandemic-schwab-survey-shows.html

4. https://assets.ctfassets.net/u7fuap5iqsvx/Yl5AJQD1mtKDM bs9V9Gj P/02d2cc5af96cb48fb74 1814f3ab7b 667/Masterworks_ Art_as_an_Investment__ Novembe r_2020_.pdf

5. http://tonsoffacts.com/25-fun-interesting-facts-starry-night-painting/

6. https://www.investopedia.com/terms/i/inflation.asp

7. https://www.cnbc.com/2021/06/10/cpi-may-2021.html

8. https://www.cnbc.com/2019/12/07/art-has-shown-long-term-returns-that-rival bonds.html

Chapter 10: Veganism & Plant-based Meat – A bright future?

1. https://thevou.com/lifestyle/2019-the-world-of-vegan-but-how-many-vegans-are-in-the-world/

2. https://www.investopedia.com/terms/e/economiesofscale.asp

3. https://www.investopedia.com/terms/s/subsidy.asp

4. https://oxfordbusinessgroup.com/news/plant-based-meat-covid-19-boom-industry

5. https://www.rush.edu/news/health-benefits-vegan-diet

6. https://theconversation.com/five-ways-the-meat-on-your-plate-is-killing-the-planet-76128

7. https://www.sciencedaily.com/releases/2016/04/160404170427.htm

8. https://www.statista.com/statistics/877369/global-meat-substitutes-market-value/

9. https://www.studyfinds.org/study-most-meat-eaters-support-veganism-but-practical-matters-keep-many-from-switching/

10. https://foodindustryexecutive.com/2019/09/companies-racing-to-introduce-plant-based-meat/

11. https://www.weforum.org/agenda/2018/12/vegetarianism-is-good-for-the-economy-too/

12. https://www.sciencedirect.com/topics/nursing-and-health-professions/cost-of-illness

13. https://news.climate.columbia.edu/2021/04/01/social-cost-of-carbon/

14. https://www.pnas.org/content/115/15/3804

Chapter 11: Quinoa - The nutritional and economic value

1. https://www.academia.edu/4144828/A_Quinoa_Fad_Wealthy_Demand_of_a_Poor_Supply_Globalized_Economic_Pressures_on_Rural_Bolivia

2. http://web.colby.edu/st297-global18/2019/01/22/superfoods-dark-side-increasing-vulnerability-of-quinoa-farmers-in-bolivia/

3. http://economicstudents.com/2016/04/the-economics-of-quinoa-superfoods-dark-side/

Chapter 12: Yoga – A storehouse of health and wealth

1. https://comparecamp.com/yoga-statistics/

2. https://www.wellnesscreatives.com/yoga-industry-trends/

3. https://runrepeat.com/gym-membership-cost

4. https://en.wikipedia.org/wiki/Diderot_effect

5. https://www.yogiapproved.com/yoga/22-celebrities-yoga-fanatics/

6. Photo by Steve Halama on Unsplash

Chapter 13: Fidget Spinners

1. https://www.theguardian.com/lifeandstyle/2017/may/03/fidget-spinner-inventor-patent-catherine-hettinger

2. https://www.nytimes.com/2017/08/15/magazine/the-rise-of-the-fidget-spinner-and-the-fall-of-the-well-managed-fad.html

3. https://www.businessofbusiness.com/articles/the-rise-and-fall-of-the-fidget-spinner/

4. https://www.livemint.com/Leisure/KK9EOl0OPw7FdDZ3aTJEKP/Do-fidget-spinners-help.html

5. https://unsplash.com/photos/188q0sVjJvk

Chapter 14: Sony Walkman – Former running champion

1. https://www.thehindu.com/news/international/the-40-year-journey-of-the-walkman/article28306111.ece

2. https://blog.oup.com/2012/07/introduction-walkman-transform-listening/

3. https://www.stuff.tv/my/features/sony-walkman-history-40-year-anniversary-malaysia-2019

4. https://startups.co.uk/blog/business-ideas-that-changed-the-world-the-walkman/

5. https://alexbrent.co.uk/culture/2019/8/15/radio-tread-how-the-walkman-changed-our-world

6. https://www.grin.com/document/132246

7. https://www.bartleby.com/essay/Disadvantages-Of-The-Middleman-Economy-F3XAV6RA4LF

8. https://unsplash.com/photos/Rks6FTfX5OU

Chapter 15: Mink Fur – Ethics vs Economics

1. https://www.theseus.fi/bitstream/handle/10024/62759/Kolokolnikov%20Andrey.pdf?sequence=1

2. https://www.reuters.com/article/us-health-coronavirus-china-mink-idUSKBN28D0PV

3. https://www.theseus.fi/bitstream/handle/10024/62759/Kolokolnikov%20Andrey.pdf?sequence=1

4. https://fashionista.com/2018/04/real-faux-fur-sutainability-ethics-debate

5. https://www.canva.com/design/DAEjT4jj0fw/oAq1xEjv9vHQIVx4z8ujHA/edit

6. https://www.wordreference.com/definition/luxury

7. https://furcommission.com/new-research-reveals-the-global-fur-trade-is-worth-as-much-as-wi-fi/

Chapter 16: Sustainable Fashion – A new eco-friendly alternative

1. https://www.worldbank.org/en/news/feature/2019/09/23/costo-moda-medio-ambiente

2. https://www.trvst.world/sustainable-living/fashion/benefits-of-thrift-shopping-for-second-hand-clothes/

3. https://www.investopedia.com/terms/f/fast-fashion.asp

4. https://unsplash.com/photos/LRqBE1z5kfE

Chapter 17: Women Empowerment – Changing social trend

1. https://www.indiaretailing.com/2019/08/30/fashion/the-changing-definition-of-womens-formal-wear-in-india/

2. https://unsplash.com/photos/K5dAn1gOFEc

3. https://unsplash.com/photos/swi1DGRCshQ

Words often associated with "Fad"

1. https://www.merriam-webster.com/dictionary/nine%20days%27%20wonder

2. https://dictionary.cambridge.org/dictionary/english/vogue

3. https://www.thefreedictionary.com/dandyism

4. https://www.thefreedictionary.com/energumen

5. https://www.merriam-webster.com/

6. https://www.thefreedictionary.com/

Characteristics of a Fad

1. https://www.encyclopedia.com/social-sciences-and-law/economics-business-and-labor/businesses-and-occupations/fads

2. https://quizlet.com/87907410/business-fads-trends-flash-cards/

Words associated with Trends

1. https://thesaurus.yourdictionary.com/trend

2. https://definition.org/define/tendency/